You may ask why?............Well, we had left England some years earlier, with our beautiful little daughter, Beverley, she was then just 4 years old.   We had found a tiny French village in the middle of a national forest, where you could see wild boar and deer running free. There was a property for sale., we wanted to live there, so to make this possible, financially, we sold everything we had, bought a shell of a house, nobody had lived in it for at least thirty years. Adjoined to the house was a barn, here we installed our caravan and started our new life.   The house was about five hundred years old, with no stairs, but that didn't matter because, there were no floors upstairs, and hardly any roof. There was one cold tap over an old sink under the broken window, and one light bulb.

Over a few years we turned it into a beautiful home. There we lived, with our wonderful French neighbours who taught us to speak the language.   There were now seven people in the village, three of them us. We had two gorgeous husky dogs and acres of fields and woods to run in, them and us........It was a dream come true, but, (there's always a but) it was so quiet. We knew that if a car came up the lane, (which ended outside our house), we would either know the people, and we didn't know many, or they were lost. Every evening we would have the same conversations with our neighbours, such as - how their dogs' nose was peeking over the edge of the bed. We drank our wine, as you do in France. It was wonderful, but, we knew we needed more, we had found heaven but it was just too soon to be there.

We applied for our Australian visas, and put our home up for sale. Years and many hours of paperwork later, we still waited......Then suddenly, still in the middle of the recession, the house sold to a South African couple.

No visas for Australia, what shall we do, should we go back to England? No!

Beverley is sitting at the table, colouring in a drawing, "Why don't we just drive there?" She exclaimed, well there's an idea, we just look at her, perhaps she's been watching too many Top Gears and Charlie Borman and Ian McGregor. We carry on discussing our options.

Then the idea came to Darren, "Let's drive to Oz while they sort our visas out." Is he serious, I thought, yes, he is! Beverleys' face said it all 'typical'!! That's when we started thinking, we have our old car, a 1991 Land Rover Defender 110. We had bought it off e-bay, for some off road fun. Why not, as Jeremy Clarkson would say "How hard can it be"?

Friday, 11 December 2009

Moving out date

We have just returned from visiting our family in the UK and we have received an email giving us our completion date, 15 Jan 2010. So that's it then, as of the 15th we are officially homeless and we start our journey to Australia. Fingers crossed all goes well.

Our first plan was to travel through Africa, we got the paint brushes, some gloss paint and we painted the Landy like a Zebra and started planning, but soon decided this was, at this time, too much of a dangerous route.

Our neighbours' faces were a picture, they were dumbfounded, having never seen anyone hand paint a car before, especially like a Zebra.

Route number two, through Europe and up to Estonia, over to Russia, keep going then turn right and down through China. So many countries to see, simple!!!!

It's getting cold now and soon the snow will arrive, so do we really want to start out in January? Perhaps at the beginning of spring, that may be a better idea? We talk to the people buying our house, they are in no rush for us to move out, we can stay till the 24th. After that, we have arranged that we can move into a friends' rental holiday home, or gite as they call it here.

Jan 21st..Jeudi.......

Have been invited by our friends, in the next village, to a farewell dinner. They say they have a big surprise for us, and indeed they have, the surprise is our neighbours are also invited, they arrive all smiles. I do love these people!!!!!

Jan 23rd....Samedi

The last farewell dinner at our neighbours! Surprise! Our friends from the next village, I cannot hold the tears back, are we doing the right thing in leaving? We have the kindest neighbours and friends, all such genuine people. We never have to lock our doors; we can leave the car keys in the ignition overnight. Will we ever find a place like this again? Well I guess it's too late now!

Jan 24th... Dimanche..

Everything we now own is either in the Landy or the trailer. James, (as we have named the Landy) stands proud, with his matching Zebra trailer and two roof tents.

Finally, and it's very sad, we leave the village for the gite--- box of tissues half empty.

What have we done?

This gite is so cold, the snow is deep and we can see it falling through the gaps around the doors. It doesn't matter how much wood we burn we cannot warm up the house.

We have just sold the warmest, centrally heated house in France and are now shivering in a gite. This house should only be occupied in the summer!!!!!!!!!!!!!

I think it's time to toughen up and get the adventurers spirit. Life has suddenly become very scary, but we all feel alive and excited.

Through the internet we have come to know another family (Agnes and Alan and their two children, June aged 9 and David---6) who are doing the same trip as us, (are they mad?).

We have decided to travel through China together. It's the law to have a Chinese guide to travel with us in the car, initial cost of £3600 and then we have to pay for all their travelling expenses, hotels, food, entrance fees, as if another member of the family. Two cars travelling together and we only need one guide, so we agree to split the cost.

A&A want to start the journey but still need to finish their house prior to rental, plumbing mainly. With Darren being a plumber, it is agreed that we will go and stay with them and help them prepare, therefore stopping us from freezing to death.

Feb 20th,

We leave the gite, I should be happy, but our dog, Alaska, is going to her new home, tears are flowing and it hurts!!!!! I know she will be better off staying in the village, she needs the freedom to run...have done it, feel so guilty separating mother and son for the first time, keep hugging Beau, he doesn't understand. I must pull myself together, they are dogs they will get over it, I'm sure I'm not really that important to them!   Bye bye

4

Cussac....bye   bye   France.............................bye   bye
Alaska................(another empty box of tissues).

Feb27th Sunday

Arrive at A&A's warm and cosy house. It's amazing how much you appreciate things, when you go without.......David comes downstairs with a sore throat, the beginning of a nasty flu, which, of course, passes to June and then Beverley..

Mercredi or Wednesday, sometimes I think in French, I suppose I shall soon forget.......Agnes is on the internet applying for visas for Russia, China, Mongolia and Kazakhstan, will leave her to it, she loves her paperwork! I'm so pleased she is so efficient at paperwork, it has taken a lot of work, and worry, away from me.

Apart from sharing germs, we have a wonderful stay at A&A's, they have made us very welcome, and given us the freedom of their house. All this time we have had Beau, our beautiful husky dog with us, he has been shedding his fur all over the house, leaving his huge footprints for all to see, you certainly know he's around, the children have made friends with him, and he with them. We are quite a family to put up for a month, they are so generous. We are all excited about our trip and spend many hours talking about it and planning. We also have had time to get to know the lovely area where they live, just across the road is the river where Beau has spent many happy hours.

31st March...

Tomorrow the journey begins, two families set off for one big adventure, scary.

Over the last few weeks we have said goodbye to so many people, many so close, some we may never see again, nobody told me it could hurt so much.

Beau has been re-homed with Beverleys' grandparents, they didn't really want a dog, but fell in love with Beau and all his charms. It's such a relief to know he will be so well looked after, couldn't have done better, although it was still so hard to say goodbye, I feel really drained, but it's my choice so can't complain.

We leave for Harwich Port at 8.15pm and arrive 10.30pm. We left A&A still cleaning their house, and I mean cleaning-----the fridge with a toothbrush, and behind the radiators the walls are sparkling, I just hope the lady renting it will keep it as clean.

April 1st Thursday! Slept in the car, it's now 6.30am, and still haven't heard from A&A (they said they would phone when they started out)

Excited! All's well !.....9.00 o'clock and we drive onto the ferry, it's huge!

 We phoned A&A, they're still in St Neots ! !! Apparently they have an appointment this morning to hand over the house keys and to have the house inspected. Therefore, it seems to me, that they had no intention of catching this ferry, but they paid for it, why? Maybe I misunderstood, shame though as Beverley is disappointed, she was looking forward to playing with her friends, what can you say, nothing stranger than people.

Good crossing, good food. I have to admit I'm glad to be arriving back on dry land. When surrounded by nothing but sea I have an underlying nervous feeling, I keep my composure, say nothing, but I'm so pleased we've landed.

Arrived at 5.00pm local time, 6.00pm in Rotterdam. As we drive along, the road is lined, both sides, with greenhouses. There is water everywhere; canals, ponds and lakes, so different! We head for

McDonalds, to use the internet, to see if we had successfully contacted Pauel. Beverley met him on our last holiday touring Europe; he lives close to where we are. Pauel and his family have travelled many miles in their converted fire truck, it's a tremendous piece of equipment, with a kitchen area and separate little bedrooms for the children. It's taken them across Africa, just to mention one place. It's now 7.00pm local time; there is no reply from Pauel.

It's very busy here so we are heading to Roosendaal, for somewhere to stop, it looks quieter on the map, we shall see!?

Friday 2nd April.

 Sunny day, 15 degrees, great night in tent at the truckers' yard (cost us 4 Euro's for 2 beers to stop there) Coffee and toilets good.

10.00am, called A&A, they are now on the ferry and want to go to Amsterdam, should arrive about 3.30pm.

10.30am and we are in Belgium heading for Antwerp.

11.30am. We must be in a Jewish area; all the people are wearing a different style of clothing. Black coats, white socks and really big, tall hats! Great to see, and very distinct. To me it feels a little like being on a film set, but this is normal life here, I have so much to learn.

There are cycle lanes everywhere, they take right of way! We have driven our first bad tarmac roads, and have paid to pass through two gigantic tunnels.

12.10pm - back in the Netherlands, we have left the main roads. We travel through villages with thatched cottages and windmills! (Sat-nav now on OFF ROAD setting) now we can see the people and countryside. This is much more fun! The land is very, very flat with thousands of wind turbines.

We are heading slowly back to Rotterdam to meet up with A&A. The weather is holding.

2.00pm, in the centre of the city. There are people on motorbikes with no helmets, it's full of activity!

Back to McD for the free Wi-Fi, and yes, Pauel has replied. We are going to meet up tonight with Karel and Sabine (his mom and dad), Pauel of course, Anika and Stille (sister and brother), and their friends, whom we met on holiday, Mary and Francis.

We have also received an email from Lukas, in Germany. We also met Lukas and his family on our last holiday. We have replied to say we will visit them in next few days--it's all or no-one!!

We waited outside the port for A&A, they followed us to McD for coffee and somewhere to park our large vehicles. We have our trailer and they, their very old caravan. I wonder how long their caravan will last, it's fragile to say the least.

Sat 3rd April---

Last night we all drove down to Pauels. Beverley is very happy to see him again, as we are. We introduce A&A and the children and they are welcomed like old friends. All the youngsters watched the Lion King 3 together, while Sabine prepared a tasty fish meal. We had a really memorable evening, chatting for hours around the table, enjoying superb food, a few bottles of wine, and such inspirational company. We hear stories of their travels around Africa, and people they have met, sights they have seen.

They have a beautiful house with goats, chickens' rabbits and cats, we slept upstairs, slept well. Had breakfast together and left about 12.30 heading for Germany.

A&A are off to Amsterdam. We will meet up again Friday 16th April, 5km east of Arad in Romania

It's exciting to think we may soon have some stories to tell of our adventures. We couldn't have been more welcomed; hope we will keep in touch.

Have just eaten a meal of mashed potato, sweetcorn and spam, delicious. Sitting at the side of the road at a place called Heure-de-Romain, OUPEYE, Belgium. We are in a layby quite near a house, so we have a chat to our new neighbours, (speaking French, proves very useful), they have no problem with us parking here, up go our tents. Just enjoying a glass of wine in the rain. --8.30 took a walk down to the village, but find nothing----8.45 last glass of wine---bed...

.

Easter Sunday 4th April—

-Woke up at 9, cup of tea, off for 10am. We have set the satnav for --Off road to Frankfurt. 11.30am and we are driving down the back streets, along the side of canal. It's interesting and funny, what a way to travel! It's 9 degrees and rainy, cosy in the Landy. We cross over two huge canals. 12.10pm and we have left Belgium, cutting across Netherlands on our way to Germany.

12.30pm and we arrive at Aachan-Germany. How many families have travelled across the world using off road satnav? Can't be many...

So far we have been to the Hoek of Holland, to Rotterdam, to Dordrecht and Antwerp, and back again. Then to Breda, Maastricht and Aachen, and are now on the way to Koblenz.

We stopped at McD for coffee + Wi-Fi, but it's not free, 8 euro per half hour, so just had coffee. Next to search for pizza, now 4pm. I have listened to the first chapter of Harry Potter, on my earphones, a really great idea!

We parked by the river at a place called Winningham, by Mosel and walked to a Pizza restaurant, which was spotted by Beverley, delicious! Next the satnav got us wedged in the middle of a market, Darren reversed out to a round of applause. There are times when I'm glad I can't see out the back window!!

7pm, and we found a lovely spot in the woods, just about to set up tents we noticed a sign warning of dangerous large ants. I don't read German, but I can understand signs with pictures! We drove on a little and found a proper parking pitch, next to a war graveyard, put up both tents and slept well. No ghosts to be seen or heard!

Monday 5th April......I have sorted out the Landy and the trailer. Darren has set the cooker up in the back of Landy, it didn't work well outside in the wind, much easier to make tea now!......11am on the road to Munich, through the woods and then some very narrow streets. The satnav says "board ferry," what? Beverley says "satnav needs to go into a mental hospital especially for insane satnavs." We have to admit it was correct, the ferry is there to cross the river. The next problem is the satnav seems to think we are driving a mini. This ferry is meant for cars, not long vehicles. Me and Beverley say "no way," but Darren says "Why not? How hard can it be?" Quite how he did it I don't know, but we're aboard. and have crossed the Rhein from Boppard to Kestert.

This is a beautiful valley stepped with vines; at a place called Lorch we see a sign, 'The Riesling Route'. There is so much traffic on these smaller roads, we think because of the bank holiday. So we have decided to go back on the motorway, for a while, to get moving.

Mainz to Karlruke--past Stuttgart to Ulm, or just underneath Ulm at a place called Laupheim, the home of Lukas, Lara, Yasmin and Finn, we last saw them in Austria, on holiday. They invited us to visit their home, I wonder if they thought we would really turn up? We should arrive about 6.30.

We arrive and park on their drive, nobody home. I start chopping onions and garlic for sauce, and cooking pasta....7.30pm Luka and Lara drive in behind the trailer. They are without the children, as they have stayed at their grandparents, shame I would like to have seen them again. I think it was a good surprise for them, they seem very happy. They insist that we sleep in their house---Lukas keeps saying "our castle is your castle"...After many beers off to bed, well when in Germany, do as the Germans do!!

Tuesday 6th

We all slept very well, although Beverley was not happy at having to sleep in a completely pink bedroom (Annas'). Lara offered me the use of their washing machine, then we put it all outside in the warm sun to dry, now 19 degrees.

Darren changed the front brake discs and pads because he is not happy, something is incorrect, then he went and had a luxurious hot shower.

Beverley, she is playing on the computer, quite content to be left alone with not a lot to say.

We all went out to lunch and had pizza (again) but we have enough left for tea, brought some bread and fresh fruit at Aldi. Then we went to see the Harley Davidson man, Nash and his wife (Darren met them last year). The bikes he is building are unbelievable; even to me, who can't tell one from another, they look spectacular. After a good look around we went and played with their five gorgeous husky dogs, (no I did not cry, even though one did have two blue eyes just like Alaska). We splash out on two T-shirts, one each for Darren and Beverley. Nash said he would try and send us the address of his aunt in Sydney and insisted we visit her.

Arrived back at Luka and Lara's about 2.30pm and told them we were off to Innsbruck. Lara says she thinks it's snowing there. It is the highest mountain in Germany and all the winter sports are on---whoops----ok, so now we are off to Salzburg.

7.30pm Whilst making sandwiches, I look up, here we are in Munich! Looking for somewhere to stop, it's all so built up! At 8pm we found a good lay-by, we heat up the pizza and make a cup of tea. Couple of chapters of audio Harry Potter, glass of wine, bed.

Wednesday 7th April,

One week in. Up at 8.30am, slept well, - on the road for 9.45. We can see mountains covered with snow! Beverley and Darren are very excited and want to get to the snow. I think I do as well, while busily thinking where the extra clothes are! 10.30am Have breakfast on the move. We put sunglasses on, and the mountains become clear against the sky---beautiful!!!! Austrian Alps wow! We are heading to Austria for lunch, we stop and eat at a restaurant, nice treat, then off again.

2.05pm The mountains are getting closer, there is a mass of snow.

3.30pm Arriving at the Austrian/Slovenian border at Villach, the satnav and the road signs say we have to go on a train. The words "how hard can it be" spring to mind again, let's go and see!!!! After some discussion and pointing of fingers at James we are allowed on the train. It takes us through a tunnel, 75km to Villach. It's still warm and sunny at 16 degrees. Here there are ski lifts and people carrying skis everywhere. As we drive we are climbing up, 970metres, my ears have gone funny! The first patch of snow on the road!...1035m---1082m and at 4.45pm. 1195metres...... Starting to go down now...753m. The brakes are cooking and steaming!! We stop for 10 minutes to cool down. The Police (Polizei) arrive to see if we are ok, no problem. We reach the bottom of the hill, still cooking, and see a sign for a campsite, thought it might be a good idea to stop for a bit, but the place is deserted, so we drive on. Found a lay-by surrounded by mountains enveloped in snow. Such an inspirational scene to cook mashed potato. We get back in James for a glass of wine and Harry Potter-----bed.

Thursday 8th April   Slept well, all warm and cosy, it must have been very cold in the night because there is condensation in the tent and we can see our breath. Toast and tea, and on the road for 9.30am. It's a warm 15degrees, the scenery is epic, unbelievable!!!! Today the agenda is breakfast in Austria, lunch in Slovenia and tea in Croatia.

Sandy the satnav has surprised me, she has taken us the other side of the mountain, completely changing the route, to what, I thought it was. Ok, so now it's 11's in Italy. We park up for a few minutes to make a great big snow ball, then walk down to river. Next we stopped at 1000 metres, at an astonishingly beautiful lake with salmon and trout.

Note to Top Gear, try and take the Predil pass and take your fishing gear!

12 o'clock Slovenia.. We reach a height of 1186 metres, before going down slowly. Stopped for cup of tea in a lay-by with a portable toilet. Three vans arrive, full of portable toilets, then a lorry with gravel for the lay-by. There are more people in this lay-by than we have seen together for ages! As we drive we see a portable toilet every couple of miles, I have never seen so many toilets.

Listening to radio Slovenia, they play a lot of English music. When they speak the language sounds Latin based, we stand a chance!

2.10pm and we are back in Italy again. A warm, sunny 24 degrees. Down to Trieste and we see the sea. 3.40pm Slovenia again-----4pm back in Italy. We are now getting a touch annoyed with the satnav. Time's getting on so we are looking for somewhere to stop. Croatia will have to wait till tomorrow.

Friday 9th April.........

We did find a lay-by and although the cars were passing us at some speed, we have all managed to have slept well. On the road for 9am --- 9.05 back in Slovenia again, bins and toilets everywhere! ---------9.45 Croatia! It crept up on us, we are so used to crossing yellow boundary lines on our map. Here there is a border control. Out come the passports, all is o.k and we pass straight through. They are literally building the road we are driving on, it's different. Today is a warm and sunny 17 degrees. We have had breakfast on the move. I would like to shop for fresh bread, do they have LIDL in Croatia? They do seem to have a Pizza restaurant every 200 yards!! We are heading for the main coast road. Spotted a shop and stopped to buy bread, they wanted Kuna, they got Euros! We all shrugged our shoulders, smiled and agreed that 20 Kuna was the correct change??

Arriving at Rijeka, it's a huge port town. Wow, it's getting hot, we are all down to T-shirts. Beverley spots a LIDL, then we see the rest, just another city!! The BBC are advertising 'Walking with dinosaurs' on large billboards. There are signs for Euros everywhere, perhaps it's a split currency at the moment. I go to the tourist information to see what they have to offer for campsites. they direct us to one. On arriving, we see that they are closed until mid-June, we are told of another.

So far we have driven 1191miles.

We are speaking a mixture of English-French-German and Italian-----it works.

  Lots of boats and cocktail bars here, there must be bags of money around. We have found the campsite--Camp Selce. It's magnificent, we are parked twenty feet from the crystal clear Adriatic. I can hear the waves lapping while I sit under a fig tree; and its warm enough for just a T-shirt.

We take a walk and buy a couple of pizzas and beers. The sea is very cold, but not cold enough to stop Beverley and Darren from jumping in, they both stood there egging each other on. I didn't think they would really do it. Beverley plunged in first, with Darren a split second after, how could they! I had to stay dry to take the photos (that's my story). Afterwards we take a hot shower, sheer luxury. Me and Beverley have managed to do the washing, there is no machine, but who cares we have hot water.

Saturday 10th April---

-Slept well---up at 7.15—Started the day with a hot cup of tea and a bacon sandwich. 9am and Beverley appears, she has been tidying her tent. It's spitting with rain so we put up the awning. It's the first time we've seen it, it's surprising we can fit the table and chairs, easily, underneath. 11am raining--11.30 still raining but I think it's passing, still warm though. Darren asked "Do you think we may have found a country without McDonalds?" It's true we cannot remember seeing one for ages. Beverley is reading to me from her book of English magic. The sun comes out so we go for walk. We find a shop and buy fruit, bread, beer and wine. We have yet another pizza and a beer, take a siesta, another walk. Whilst watching a stunning sunset, we get chatting with a couple from Malaysia, lovely people, they give us their phone number, and address, and ask us to call in as we pass through their country. It's getting windy now, a passing Croation couple seem to be trying to tell us that we are going to fall into the sea? Must be a big storm coming!

Sunday 11th April-----

The strong winds lasted all night, Beverley slept through it all! It battered us all night long, but we still didn't fall into the sea! 1 nil to us! This morning is sunny and warm, but so windy. We have decided, that as we will probably end up sitting in the car, not much else we can do in these winds, might as well move on.

Midday on the road again, this time heading for Lake Balaton in Hungary. 1pm and we have just driven up the steepest hill ever, to the top of a mountain, to be met by a snow blizzard. Again, the road is being built as we drive on it. The sheer drops off the side of the road make my stomach curdle each time I glance down at them. It's nerve racking, especially on the bends when you don't know if someone else is coming the other way. We really didn't expect to see these conditions until we reached further east.

We passed through a bridge dated 1945 with a hammer and sickle on, thoughts of war and Russia creeping through me, very spooky! It's freezing cold and snowing--now hailing! Yuk! It was my stupid idea to leave the sunny seaside! Now it's changed into a very heavy snow storm.

2.10pm and we drove out of the storm heading towards Slovenia. The suns out and it's getting warmer. I am just starting to feel a bit easier when we get stopped at the border. Darren is severely questioned "why carry diesel, why no cigarettes, what are those things on the roof? " etcetera.

I wonder if when I was a child, I watched too many war films. I can remember Doctor Zhivago. It's just that Russian type uniforms and freezing cold weather seem to have a frightening effect on me?

 Anyway here we are back in the land of the portaloo, as Darren calls it, heading for Ljubljana on road number 106. We are keeping a close eye on Sandy satnav, because we don't want to go back to the Croatian border control again.   The satnav is behaving, all seems well. 4.45pm we stop for a cuppa at Lukovica, north of Ljubljana, in the local café. Darren spots a sign on the wall   'Walkers exhausts.' These were made in Tyseley in Birmingham, England, the world suddenly feels smaller.

Lots of the houses here are brightly painted, lime green, pink and orange. Sometimes all these colours on the same house. It's as if coloured paint has just arrived, perhaps it has.

 We find a lay-by hidden behind several trees, our home for the night. I cook mashed potato, noodles and sweet corn. We watch the film 'The Time Machine', with a glass of wine, then to bed.....

Monday 12th April....

Thoughts of my family, as this is a special day   I tell myself that's enough of that, can't contact them, toughen up!

Slovenia at 8am , and it's stopped raining, just long enough to fold down the tents. On the road for 9.30 and we go straight to ALDI supermarket (they are everywhere) and also Spar. We buy bread, fruit, vegetables, beer and wine. I always try and keep enough food to last us several days, perhaps a week or so, it stops me worrying, well you never know what's going to happen.

It's raining again, really miserable today. 11.35am and we popped into Austria again...11.41am and we're back in Slovenia. At 11.55am we are at place called Munska Sobota. Here there is a road diversion sign, and then a low bridge 2.5metres. This causes us grief as we cannot pass under it. We drive around town, but there is no other way out, there must be for lorries, but we can't find it. Back to the bridge, Darren has had enough, he decides to try it. There are height strips hanging down and we touch them, we just scrape through. We think, at last we can get out of this town, then Sandy satnav took us to a factory car park and told us to drive into the factory!! Ignoring this advice, Darren finds his own way out of town. Next we passed through a town called Fokovci, well, with that name it had to have a mention!

1pm and we crossed the border into Hungary, no one at the border! Stopped to buy Beverley a new coat, but the bank card would not work. We drove to Keszthely and changed a bit of cash, Euro for Florint. Looking for a phone box, to phone our bank, we are soaked, it won't stop raining – yuk. We notice a Tesco and McD. We find the phone box, but it will not take the money, it's still raining, everywhere is closed. This is the lowest part of our trip, so far.

We managed to get an internet connection for a few minutes and received an e-mail from A&A to say they won't get to Arad for another week.   As we drive we cannot see lake Balaton, it is completely obscured by closed businesses and fences. Darren cooked dinner, while Beverley read to me and did a bit of writing. Sitting in the Landy and just talking, it's good. Beverley says she is going to have a series Landrover and a fire truck, which she will convert into a huge camper van. Cosy and comfortable, and I accidently drop my can of beer and it pours all over me, clever eh! What a day...

Tuesday 13th April

Slept well. It's still raining, and so gloomy. We are on the road for 10am. Stop for a cuppa, and we speak to a local who stopped to say that he is very interested in what we are doing. He told us there is no personal freedom in Hungary any more, and it was good to see people travelling where they want. It makes me think about how lucky we are to have the freedom to do this trip.

Darren went to Tesco and bought a phone charger, phoned visa, and got the bank card working again, all for the bargain price of 1195 florint (£6.50).

11am and off we go to the Slovak Republic. We saw another Tesco and stopped to spend the rest of our Hungarian cash. 12.45 still raining, 2pm rain seems to be clearing.

We stopped 41 km from Gyor and crossed into Slovakia at 3pm. By 3.45pm we are thinking, perhaps we should have gone to Romania, we don't like it here. It's still raining.

So we drove onto Sturovo, where we stopped at a pizza bar. Here we were able to connect to the internet and send our e-mails. Afterwards we found a lay-by and set the tents up. I listened to Mr. Potter, glass of wine, then bed.

Wednesday 14th April........Slept well, on the road for 9am. It's just stopped raining, hurray! We have decided to head south for Arad in Romania. 9.02 into Hungary---9.06 back in Slovakia. Talking in the car, the question arose, as to how many countries we had visited so far. We have a count up, Holland-Belgium-Germany-Croatia-Italy, Hungary-Austria-Slovak rep. and Slovenia--- that's nine so far.

11.30 just leaving Budapest, in the rain, another busy city, not my kind of place, dreadful, although quite interesting. 11.40 and it's stopped raining!!!!! 12.20 Sun--wow--first for days. Unfortunately, we will remember Hungary for rain, Tesco and lots of ladies with bright red hair. (I'm sure it is lovely in the summer). 2pm and it's looking a lot brighter. We are halfway to Arad with the sun shining. We keep seeing dogs in the middle of nowhere, they appear to be living at the side of the road, we've seen four or five, sitting alone, nothing and no-one for miles, strange. We stopped to buy bread at a tiny co-op in Szentey , the people were so friendly. We bought 6 rolls and a big loaf, it cost us 369 florints, about £1.50. The weather is still dry with tiny patches of blue sky and sun. We are having fun trying to pronounce the place names. The land is very flat and open, the roads are boneshakers, so many potholes, I'm glad we are in the Landy!! Everywhere we look we see machines digging for oil, believe they are called donkeys.

3.20pm and we are leaving Hungary. We are all stopped for a police check, passports all ok. Then at 3.30pm (the time changed to 4.30pm) we entered Romania and were stopped by customs who checked our passports and papers, all ok. Then we drove straight to a garage to buy a vignette, in Romanian it's a Rovineta, in English it's road tax, about £3 per week.

The land is very flat, there are no fences with sheep everywhere, it looks very bleak. More oil donkeys, then a surprise! Within minutes we come to a large shopping complex with a Carrefore--Bricostore--Intersport, the same as in France. We stopped to get some cash, me and Beverley stay with the car. Darren returns and says it is the largest shopping complex he has ever seen. Apparently, you can buy anything and half of it is English, we were not expecting that!!! A few minutes later we arrived in Arad, it is easily as busy as London with crazy drivers and trams and horns and hundreds of people. It makes my toes curl with all this traffic, Darren says "Like driving in Paris" nothing bothers him. This is really not how we imagined Romania to be!! We see more and more shopping complexes, an advert says 'house and land 50,000 euro' ooh no thanks. It's absolute chaos, I think there must be loads of money around. It's pouring with rain again!!! The signs have a lot of French and Italian in them, so we can make out quite a bit. 6.15pm, still raining, the road is still very busy, but getting a bit better.

We spot a camp site.......

Thursday 15th.

Slept well, and it's 10.30! Well the clocks have been changed on us, it's not raining and the sun is trying to come out. On the hill above us there is a creepy, spine chilling castle, superb.

We will move on today, the camp-site is fine, but no showers or washing facilities. It's next to a large river, which at first looks lovely, but as you watch you can see plastic bottles floating, I can count ten at a time! Darren went to pay for our stay but they would not take any money, so we gave them a bottle of champagne, which we still had from England, it brought a smile.

We don't know where to go for Draculas castle----we were supposed to meet A&A tomorrow. They have all the guide books and the dongle connection for the internet. They sent a message to say they will not be arriving for another week. We will find a way by ourselves, who needs books and internet, there are people here!

1.30pm, it is beautiful here in the mountains (although it has started raining again), except for the rubbish, it's everywhere!! Mainly plastic, it seems to be swallowing up the countryside.

We are looking at the forests and the mountains and talking about how there are still bears and wolves living here. It all sounds very exciting, but this is real, it's not a fairy tale. We had better watch where we camp tonight!!! There are sheep everywhere and each group has a shepherd, well, that proves the wolf theory....

Passing through the towns, one thing that stands out, is the gas pipes, they are all above ground. It's a complete mess to my eyes. They run along the side of the roads, when they come to a driveway, it's up and over, forming a huge rectangular entry point. The roads are a bit of a mess too, with the amount of holes in them. There are many people hitch-hiking. When we stopped at a garage, a man with a baby in his arms, came over to us begging for money. At first glance they looked sad, but we soon felt threatened. Darren told him where to go, at first he just continued ranting, he understood better when Darren showed him his machete!!

7.15pm. This is more like it, we are wild camping. Sitting around the campfire cooking dinner. Beverley is busy making a big wooden stake (with the pen knife we bought last year in Switzerland), ready for the vampires tonight. Scary, so is the thought of wolves!!!! We are camped at the side of a river, where we have found some really strange bones, covered in beetles, something has been killed here by something! We are next to the forest, and it's becoming dusk. I wonder if we will have any visitors tonight! Beverley was going to bed, in the pitch black, except for the torch, when we both heard strange noises. That does it, tonight we all sleep together in one tent!

Friday 16th

. Slept well, (no vampires or wolves). We have lit a fire and put a joint of pork to cook in our (French) Dutch oven, we've covered it in as much burning wood as we can, will await the outcome...We had decided to stay here for a day, it's really pleasant and the sun is shining, and of course, it's free. Then we have a visitor, a Romanian man on his bike, seemed really friendly. His bike was equipped with almost everything you could need. Strange that he said he didn't have a pump and could he borrow one. Darren tried to help but our pump was no good for his bike. After he left Darren said, and we agreed, it was time to move off, the man was just too suspicious, all that equipment and no pump? Darren had also noticed that his tyre was quite firm. We packed up, a few miles up the road we saw the man cycling, perhaps he was ok, we will never know!

As we drive, there are so many horses, standing and walking over the roads, we also saw one being carried on the back of a pickup truck. As we are climbing up another mountain road, the forest is getting thicker and thicker, then all of a sudden we arrive at a cement works!!! We have to say that this country is definitely full of surprises. Next is the town of Zlatra, yuk, there are slums everywhere you look. Half built, or maybe, condemned, buildings with no windows or doors, are being lived in. Darren says "Now I can understand the border guard, when he asked me why we wanted to visit Romania?" I feel quite scared here, just what does a car painted like a zebra look like to these people.

There is no trouble as we pass through, I feel guilty for having being scared. Seems I'm the only one with bad thoughts.

Further on, and another town Alba Lulia. There are new houses everywhere, we think there must be heaps of money here. 3.30pm we pass an old shepherd wrapped in blankets, just sitting there watching his sheep. The traffic is crazy, the drivers take a lot of risks, and in-between them, are the horse and carts, you can see an accident about to happen every minute. Somehow they get away with it, such a mixture of people!! I guess this is the norm to them. Darren says "I'm watching articulated lorries dodging potholes, on a motorway, at speed--love this place it's starting to grow on me"...We see yet another McD and signs for the Hilton Hotel. I mentioned that the Hotel sounded rather nice, but nothing happened. Drove on till we found another road side wild camping area, seems to be all there is here, (apart from the Hilton). The river water looks clean, so me and Beverley wash a bucketful of clothes. It's hard work, and the cold leaves your hands numb, but there is something very satisfying about it. After that we ate the ribs of pork we had cooked in the Dutch oven, it had worked perfectly…...fantastic, beats TGI Friday's any day!!!! We watched Pirates of the Caribbean 3 on the lap-top---glass of wine------bed.

Saturday 17th April.

There was a massive storm in the night, apart from that we slept well and awoke to warm sunshine. During the night we had visitors of the unwanted kind. We had owned a four- part ladder, which Darren used every day to help put up the roof tents, now there is only one part! Some of our washing has gone and the washing line cut. Me and Beverley had washed quite a load in the freezing cold river, now most of it is on the muddy floor. Never mind it could have been a lot worse! We were going to stop for the day, but now are going to move on, we think it wiser.

On the road for midday, we are going to try and find the Transfagarasan highway, we first saw this on Top Gear, a magnificent piece or work, that snakes its way up, over and down the mountains, if they can do it, so can we!

We pass lots of really tiny stalls selling cheeses and bread, and in contrast a Great Western Hotel with a limo on the drive. A man sitting in a field, with no fences, by the side of the road, watching his cows. We see people working the land with horses, a man shepherding his goats on the railway line.

We see many houses, which to me at first sight, with my un-travelled eyes, I have called slums. I'm learning that these are peoples' homes and I have no right to name them in such a way. We are living in a car; how does that appear at first sight? Also they do seem to all have satellite dishes, we haven't got one!

1.30pm turned off towards the mountains, covered in snow. This is it, we have found the highway, passing through the last marked village on the map. The mountain is marked as 2254m, that's pretty high! I don't know if I am looking forward to this climb, it's exciting, but it's going to be very cold. At 500m, the trees are full of mistletoe, we recognise that from France. 670m there are signs suggesting the use of snow tyres, and chains. The sun is still shining but it's getting very windy. At 800m the trees grow thickly together, some areas are being felled....935m- we're yawning, the air is getting thinner......1000m it's just corner after corner---1074m stopped to let engine cool down.....1113m the snow begins.......1255m... the road is blocked,-- it has collapsed. What a disappointment. Darren has to reverse very slowly, whilst turning. I find this scary, but I am the only one! I'm glad when it's over!! Such a shame, to be stopped in this way, half way across this famous highway, not to see the top or the south-side......oh well, there's nothing we can do to change it.

Onto Dracula Castle in Bran, Transylvania!! 4.20pm and we are getting close. Here there are oxen and carts, with cows walking alongside. It's like going back in time, apart from everyone is on their mobile phones. We see a horse and cart with a coffin in the back, 5.20pm and we are

6km from Bran. We stop at a shop for, amongst other things, our beer supply, me and Beverley go in. The local people are all smiles and seem genuinely pleased to serve us.

Sunday 18th April.

Yesterday evening, as we drove excitedly into Bran, we saw a sign that said 'Vampire Camping', we turned and drove in. Could this really be a proper campsite? Yes - hot showers, washing machine and Wi-Fi - luxury!! Settled in and went to bed at 9.30pm. Woke up at 9.30am, we had slept a full 12 hours!!! The sun is shining and I heard a cricket singing, I love this time of year when they start singing, it means summer will soon be here. We have been following spring since we started out, the Dandelions have been just starting to flower for the whole journey. This was something I had not thought about; I wonder if it will continue as we drive up towards Russia? It could be the longest Spring we will ever see.

Tony, the man who runs this site, lives here with his wife, he speaks English and is very friendly and helpful. Darren asked him if we could use his address to send off for our Russian visas. (We couldn't do this before, because, the visas don't last very long, but they begin as soon as they are issued, therefore, we would not have time to cross Russia before they ran out.) He said yes, and, as he was going to town tomorrow, he would see to the correct postage for us. So now we all have to do is wait for our paperwork to be returned to us. Fingers crossed there are no problems, as we are in a foreign country without passports, I don't want to have to try and explain that one.

After having showers and doing the washing, it's time to walk up to the castle.

It looks impressive, even distinguished. Built, perched, on the hilltop, with the backdrop of the Carpathian Mountains. It towers above the town, unnervingly, suggesting a link with the mystical, and the gothic horror tales of Bram Stoker. After seeing many photographs, movies and talking about this castle, it feels like quite an achievement to be here. One above Mr. Stoker who apparently never actually came here.

24

It is 4pm and it closes at 6pm, so we make the decision to go inside tomorrow, and not have to rush. All around the castle are stalls with all the usual tourist items that you would expect. Dracula mugs, swords, weapons, castle playing cards, just about anything you could think of. Alongside all of this paraphernalia, on nearly every stall we were also offered a selection of Hannah Montanna items, she gets everywhere! So we had a walk around, bought a couple of pizzas and a beer and coke, then back to base camp.

The sun is shining and I am sitting here in a T-shirt. We will be staying here for a while, it's good not to have to pack up, makes a change. Darren is lying on the bench moaning that he hasn't got a beer and Beverley is on the computer, drawing, whilst listening to Harry Potter. In the field with us are sheep, they have bells on, it's a very pleasant sound, I watch as they start to wander towards the gate, the shepherd gives one whistle and they run to him, just like well trained dogs, they have three lambs with them--ahh so cute.

7pm and there is only one other caravan on the site, and the people are getting ready to leave. Tony comes over and asks if we would like eggs and cheese from the shepherd/farmer, why not......We now have twenty fresh eggs and a whole homemade cheese, which is huge, and delicious, a bag full of apples, all for £6.50, can't complain about that!! Looking at our table we notice we have, cheese and eggs from Romania---cheese from Hungary--bread from Germany--vegetable oil from France--wine for Slovenia---margarine from Tesco, England and chilli oil from Thailand. The chilli oil we actually brought in France and it has travelled with us since we left, we will probably take it back to its home in Thailand....

Monday 19th....

Slept well, woken by noises, Darren said he saw a large wolf like dog-or wolf-we don't know, it was trying to get into one of the bins.

Today we are going to do a lot of walking, so we start with bacon and egg for us, Weetabix for Beverley, then off to Bran Castle. We climb the hill approaching the grounds and pass the myriad of souvenir shops, through the innumerable stalls to the entrance. Once inside there are a few more select craft stores, selling musical instruments, hats and clothes. Past these and we come to the grounds keepers house. The roof is covered in moss and the place is in disrepair. Darren is instantly taken by the building, he explains in some detail how he would repair it, given the chance. We climb the many tiny steps to the entrance, what a view!

The castle interior is immaculate. Carved wooden doors open onto polished wooden floors, with period furniture. One of the bedrooms has a four poster bed, absolutely gorgeous, the carving is so intricate. The whole of the castle is heated with a fireplace in each room. It's all resplendent, and built into the centre is a closed in courtyard.

3pm. The visit was really satisfying, as Beverley said "It was indeed a pleasurable experience," and Darren "Big and high with so many tiny steps"....Yes, there was plenty to look at and read about Vlad the impaler and of course Dracula----great fun. Again we pass through the souvenir shops, this time Darren managed to talk Beverley into buying a T-shirts. It was only £5 but Beverley insisted she could make one for less, she wouldn't buy anything else! Finished with a picnic in castle grounds.

Temp is 20 degrees---Darren changed a wheel bearing, I re-arranged the Landy again, there was so much stuff on top of the fridge it wouldn't open....Beverley reading and drawing....6.45pm Darren and Beverley both reading. It's raining outside, hope it's just tonight......Tony sent the passports today, so now we wait! Should be about 10 days.........

Wednesday 21st April.

Up at 7am. Last night, we had a visitor, of the four legged variety, bins emptied, the cheese has gone, I had put it in a sealed box, footprints all over table.

8am sun comes out--it's a beautiful day, I can see the snow top mountains they are shining!! Off to Brasov today, with directions from Tony, to a shop called Hornbach, to buy new ladder and padlock.

Very successful, we got everything we wanted. Driving around Brasov we saw the usual Carrefour and McDonalds, then Darren spotted The Royal Bank of Scotland, we were not expecting that one. Stopped at traffic lights, they all have countdown timers on them, good idea. This is a huge town, with lots of second hand shops? People just walk out into the road, sometimes on crossings--sometimes not, and they don't even glance at the traffic. Beverley says that explains why they have such large graveyards, good point! There are white taxis everywhere, and people sweeping the roads with witches' brooms. We have noticed today that the horse and carts have number plates.

On our way back to the tent we stop at the local supermarket called 'Wolf'---Darren bought a cheap hair dye for £2. He put the die on, then took his blue shirt off, wiping it across his head, now he has blond hair with blue streaks (his first blue rinse) he likes it!

Thursday 22nd.

 Showery day, so we set up our big tv and the wii----watched Dr. Who (thanks again Grandad)---lazy day.

Friday 23rd April.

  Went back to Bran castle and took it slowly--sat and watched the town through the high windows, it was enjoyable. As we were leaving Agnes and Alan drove past us, unbelievable!!! We walked back down to our campsite, and they were there. We have driven two and a half thousand miles and we end up on the same site! Good to see Beverley playing with June and David. We all had dinner together then played scrabble, checked e-mails and, great news, the passports have arrived at our agents, who are called Real Russia---phew!

Sat 24th

Up at 9.30--it's just stopped raining--the sun is trying but it's a bit of a grey, overcast day. Beverley, June and David watched films. Again, we all had dinner together, played scrabble--glass of wine---bed.

Sun 25th, much the same as yesterday, decide to leave for the Black Sea tomorrow....

Monday 26th April

It's sunny and hot! Pack up, leaving our trailer on site and set off---.... We see a man talking on his mobile phone whilst driving his horse and cart--well why not, but it does look odd, it's two different worlds! We see roadside stalls selling immense amounts of plastic items, best described as unnecessary, gnomes, dancing flowers, balls. Before long there is a hotel--then another stall, and so on. We drive through a town called Ploiesti. All along the roads there are wells for water. Darren has noticed that nobody in Romania wears glasses, so of course now, that is what we are looking for, 'spot the glasses' seems to be true, can't see any! As the miles go past, we now see wells every hundred yards or so!

Last night stayed in a campsite, it had not opened for the season, but they didn't mind. It was by the side of a small lake and the bull frogs were singing, really loudly, hearing them was just like being back in France!! Three or four dogs around--as usual, we have two names for them that they all seem to fit---Limpy or Infectie dog!

Wednesday 28th

Here we go again, today the land is so flat and open--lots of rape seed-- the animals are changing, it's now goats instead of sheep and there seems to be a lot of donkeys...

Thursday 29th.

We want to go back to wild camping and have found a lovely spot, on top of a cliff. Beautiful sea views, lovely sandy beach. Me and Beverley have collected shells, and paddled in the sea. We walked around the cliffs, and noticed that the place is starting to open up, people are arriving to open up the bars. We are told that, this week-end there is to be a big party on the beach for 'Workers day'.

Date???? Started to write this thinking its Friday the 30th but the computer says its Thursday 29th--very confusing, I have no idea how I have jumped a day, but the good thing is it really doesn't matter--it makes no difference.........

Friday 30th April.

Last night we sat around our campfire talking to our neighbours- two bikers--Holger (German) and Anne (polish) and the caravanetters Pascal and Cécile (Swiss). Anne gave Beverley a collection of shells from the beach. The party on the beach, now in full swing, in fact it went on all night till the sun came up.

Collected wood with Pascal and Cécile, for tonight is the night of the witches, and the tradition is a big bonfire! Hot sun shining now. A big stage has been built on the beach, there are literally thousands of people down there. Lots have walked up on to the cliff top and taken our photo as they passed. Cécile has given Beverley a penknife with an attachment that will (with a bit of effort) make holes in the shells--- Beverley has spent hours making a necklace and anklet... Met Susie and Tomas--from Germany and Slovakia, they are both in their 20's and have been on the road for a year in their van.... sat around camp fire and talked, brilliant!!

Saturday 1st May

Just chilled today...on the night we met Adrian and Andrew----two young Romanians, we had a good laugh with them; talking around the fire. Every time Adrian spoke, he quoted some-one, his favourite being Salvador Dali. Darren kept asking him "what does Adrian think" answered with "well Dali said", eventually Darren told him it was like talking to Wiki-f***ing-pedia, the laughter was extreme, slowly Adrian began to catch on that we were only interested in him not Dali!!

2nd----Left Vama Veche (old border) and drove to the Danube Delta at Tulcea...hilly...very lush green...23 degrees-----parked up for night next to trees standing in water.

3rd-----went on ferry across delta...back into mountains towards Brasov, arrived back at Vampire camping to find trailer safe and well.

4th----...Spent most of the day reorganising the Landy and trailer again, and washing. We got the summer clothes out, and put the awning up. It's lovely, it's too hot to sit in the sun, this I like! Beverley sorted out some books from the trailer and sat reading for ages. At about 11am thousands of little black flies appear, they don't do any harm just hover around for a couple of hours, mating, then disappear.

  It has changed here since our last visit--the trees have blossomed, a little less snow on the mountain top, and the forests have filled out, there is so much vegetation it's dark in there....

5th----Beverley busy writing, Darren reading.....Frank a biker from Germany has come over for a chat, he has travelled all over the world, we exchange stories for a while...today we chill!

6th----To Savata---north to the salt lake and cave, rain, rain and more rain. There is nowhere to wild camp. 1st campsite closed-2nd horrible--3rd great----hello Frank---eventually it stopped raining--

7th- May. Beautiful morning, went for walk for a few hours. Another pizza, best yet! It's still warm but stormy with rain and thunder.

8th----Drove to man-made lake at Bicaz, and drove through a canyon, it was stunning. We couldn't get down to the lake, then we saw a sign 'zone touristica', it turned out to be a closed, falling down factory. They said we could camp there, but me and Beverley said no, it was horrible, it looked like a rats' paradise!! We wild camped, by the side of the road, built a big fire with Frank, he gave Darren a knife as a gift.....many passers-by toot their horns and wave at us.......

9th----Goodbye Frank....we went back through the gorge again; it was that breath-taking. We parked to look over the side of a dam, looked down, we saw what, at first, looked like a beach but it was entirely made up of plastic bottles, well they are being collected, that's good. Back to Bran....

10th May

Set off for another attempt at the Transfagaran Highway. Fabulous alpine roads--25 degrees....start to climb--845m still warm--loads of wild camping spots--edges of road collapsed--very bumpy--lorries full of logs----sheer drops--waterfalls---then a long drive, road is twisty but normal---forest is very thick--first bits of snow, then the road opens up, the forest just ends and you can see all the snow---the road is narrow, the snow has been cut through, on the inside it is as high as the Landy, on the outside sheer drops....we come to a place that it is possible to turn round, we all agree it's far too dangerous to continue, it's just not worth it, we know its blocked further on...so we take the photos and drive down just below the snow to find a pitch for the night......

11th----Slept well on pitch next to river, then moved further down the mountain to the lake for a quiet day. No driving today. This is a beautiful open pitch---we saw only 3 cars all day, one stopped to take a photo of us for his fishing magazine.

12th-----Spent the day walking and exploring, we found newts and leeches in small pools. Another night by the river, quite interesting. The night was absolutely pitch black, we started to hear noises. After a while Darren decides to climb down from the tent to have a closer look, braver than me! It was wild horses; they had come to see what on earth we were.

13th- May

We were out of bed at 5am to get out of the tents and into the car--the storm was overhead—and we were the only metal thing halfway up the mountain! Rain lashing down, strong winds and lightening was enough to scare anyone, it did a good job on me! When it was over we sct off down the mountain, wet and cold. The road was a mess, flooded in places and there had been rock falls. This was far scarier than going up!! Heading back to Bran we passed a ruined castle which was supposed to be the proper Dracula castle, Darren and Beverley climbed the 1400 steps to have a look, I decided to guard the car!   Arrived back at Bran to find our passports had arrived........

14th We finally left Vampire camping.   Off to visit the other Dracula castle at Sighisoara.   We are not impressed with this one, boring compared to Bran. We continue further to a camp site at Cluj Napoca. As we drove Beverleys' guitar, which had been attached to the trailer, fell off and smashed, real shame. At the camp, Darren checked the car and changed all the tyres around, me and Beverley caught up with the washing.

15th----To Oreadea on the Romanian-Hungarian border.   It's time to leave Romania, we've been here so long we've stopped converting the money, we're so used to it. The clocks go back an hour. It's rain-rain-rain, all the fields are flooded.

Three hours later at 5pm, arrive at Hungarian-Slovak border. Just as we enter there is a big bump in the road and the trailer hitch snaps clean off--we've blocked the border!!! Luckily we are undercover. Darren managed to drag the trailer across the .road and out of the way. The border guard comes and has a look and checks us out. Two cars pass through the border, the guard stops one. He is a mechanic, a friend of the guard. He comes and has a look at our situation, then drives off. Soon he returns with his welding gear. An hour and a half later we are back on the road---truly kind, meeting people in this way really lifts your spirits.

Sunday 16th May

Rain-rain and more rain. Slovakia is much cleaner than Romania. They have rivers with no plastic bottles. Every few miles there is a Tesco, we have just bought a new phone card from one, at the top of a mountain. 12.30 the sun is trying to come out, we all have wet feet and trousers, it's pretty horrible!!

Decide to drive to Czech Republic, and visit a monastery, I have read it is famous for its collection of human bones. Have just passed a warning sign that said 'Bears-wild horses-wolves-deer' bit scary!

4.35pm and we arrive at the border. No customs or stops, just a sign. It's still raining heavily, we find a sheltered spot, off the road in the trees.

17th---Just drizzling----drove into centre of BRNO and bought a jockey wheel for the trailer for 1080 korunas (about £30) now we just need someone to weld it on and reinforce the hitch. It's very clean here with lots of recycling bins.

Arrived at Blansko, can't see any signs for the monastery, but we found tourist information. Me and Beverley go in and explain what we are looking for, the lady spoke good English, so that part was easy. It appears we have the wrong Blansko--"We don't have bones here, just a wooden church," she wasn't very impressed with us!!!

We can't find a map to buy, and have no internet connection, so it's back to Slovakia, because Darren had seen an off road centre, and thought that would be the best place to get our repairs done. ..

18th- May

Camped outside a pizza restaurant, in the car park, the camp sites are flooded. Our tent has leaked, all our bedding is soaked, luckily we have spare sleeping bags, and Beverley let us sleep in her tent. We drove on looking for off road centre and found it!!! Left the trailer to be picked up tomorrow. Went and bought new sleeping bags and blow up pillows.

 Climbed a mountain and went into the ice caves, brilliant. Afterwards we found our first Hotel, and had hot baths--our first since January-19th.

Drove to find a place to open up the tents to dry out. Saw wooden church built 1746, it's an unesco site. Then we saw a huge bonfire made from logs, in the shape of a pyramid (we think Wicker Man, you know, Edward Woodward)---off we go!

Picked up trailer, they have done great job 160 euros....Next we drive to a thermal spring that Tomas, (party on the beach) told us about. It's amazing, all this hot water, bubbling up out of the ground, free. I wonder how long before a fence goes up.

Thursday 20th

-Set out for Poland...counting England this is our thirteenth country.

We can't get through the mountain passes. Roads closed, flooded. The satnav sends us up an unpaved road, scary, she doesn't know what she's doing, so we decide to ignore sandy satnav and go on the main roads only!! Grey sky, rain, rain and water everywhere--river banks collapsed--fields flooded--sand bags everywhere.

Arrived at Oswiecim (Auschwitz) at 5.30pm----camped nearby at truckstop, which is smelly due to piles of rubbish, but hey, just one night!

21st- May

Auschwitz......it's impossible to put our feelings into words, you have to see for yourself, The sights we have seen and the stories we have been told will stay with us forever. So much suffering, it makes you feel ashamed to be human. Photographs along the walls of those poor people, their eyes seem to follow you, hope it's not too much for Beverley. We have done the main tour, it continues on, but we have had enough. Don't want to see or hear anymore.

To Krakow it's the only open way to get to the north, we head for the small desert, we have heard about, at Olkusz, to camp. We see rivers flooded and bridges destroyed, such devastation.

On the brighter side, we also see Aldi--Tesco and McDonalds.

22nd-

Wake up feeling dizzy, my legs are very wobbly, perhaps because of the bad dreams after yesterdays visit. It's weird, I have never felt like this before. Keep seeing and thinking about Auschwitz, I'm pretty sure it has shocked my system to the point of physically reacting How did people survive that place and then continue to live, I feel such admiration for them.......Stop thinking, time to move on ....

Sitting next to desert enjoying a rest, and we are asked to move on, very politely by police. We get bogged down in the sand, and had to dig the Landy out. Good practice for the Gobi.

We reached 100 km from Warsaw and stopped at a lay-by. We watch in amazement, as a car parks by us, four people jump out, drink a whole bottle of vodka, in just minutes, then drive off again.

Back to thunderstorms, again!

23rd-----8am more people arriving for drinks!!!! 8.30am we are off. The Landy is not happy, the UJ's are squeaking and making horrible noises. Darren stops and greases them, all ok now. See more sand bags and rivers flooded ...the sun is shining its 22 degrees!!! 50k from Warsaw and its orchards everywhere with bits of blossom still in trees. And dandelions! 10k from Warsaw and we start to notice English words appearing, such as 'For Sale'. We see a huge Ikea--McD--KFC., any shop you can think of, but all closed today. Even the 24 hour 7 day Tesco is closed.

Driving north, past Warsaw, to Bialstok. We pull over to stop, the spring on the trailer has broken. It will still tow, but we are not very happy. There are mosquitos everywhere-----drive to hotel and write this..

24th May

We have searched for a motorcycle shop for a new spring, no luck in town, so started out for Lithuania. Sandy satnav took us the quiet way through the countryside. We saw cows with their front legs roped together like handcuffs (nasty to see). Miles and miles of forests, with the ground covered with lily of the valley, beautiful.

3.pm and country number 14. Lithuania, no stops at border just a wave. My first impression is, it looks very clean and tidy. We found a decent parking spot, off road, with a sheer drop down to a river. The dandelions have just finished flowering. A chap stopped for a chat, an RAF officer. He told us where to look for a motorbike shop, and gave us his phone number in case we had any problems, isn't that kind!

Tuesday 25th May

Sunshine and showers. To Kaunas, to buy a spring. It's a neat and tidy city, no motorbikes to be seen!! We found the shop but no good, they don't have what we need.

We are off to the seaside. We see many wooden houses made of larch, some painted, others natural. Some made of small bricks, the colour of sandstone. We found a campsite at Vente, called Camp Ventaine, and as the name says it is just too windy. The site is pleasant, so we will stay one night. We walked onto the beach to see the Baltic sea, it looks browny-grey--yuk--not inviting and very rough!!!

26th---

-Off to find a new camping pitch. The trees here are still full of blossom. Arrived at Klaidepa , again, there are no motorbikes to be seen. This place has many jewellers, hairdressers and casinos. Rain, rain and rain. Off to try Latvia, arrived at 4.30pm, no there are no bikes here!! Now heading for Riga, with the sun shining--passed through and found a camp -site by a lake--beautiful--£3 per night!!!

27th---stayed day and night.

28th-May.

 We have moved up the coast a bit and found miles and miles of white, sandy, empty beaches. 1.40pm and it's ' hello Estonia,' again no stop at the border. Looks clean and tidy, there is a sign for reindeer! Drove up to Parnu, and we found a motorbike shop, but no good, they said they could order a spring but it would take about two weeks!! Parked up on the grass ,next to the beach, no-one else is around here, our own private beach, fantastic. If the weather holds we will stay here a day or oo we cannot enter Russia before the 1st of June.......

Saturday 29th May.

It was very cold last night, the moon was very low in the sky. The weather today is ok, but not warm enough for the beach, so off we go to to Tallin. Still only one or two motorbikes and no bike shops. We continue on to the sea—we see a sign for St.Petersburg 323km. Today we have seen only one animal, a dog--but no sheep, no cows, nothing. The trees are in blossom and dandelions are flowering. Every house we see is different, never two the same. Arrived at a place called Kunda, we were hoping for sea side, but there is none, just factories, we were hoping for a beach, but this place is just a nightmare of concrete, 6pm and nowhere to stop, sides of roads are all drainage ditches and bus stops. It's another two hours before we find a pitch!!

3oth May.

We are backtracking, again, because Darren saw a Jaguar breakers and thinks they may have a suitable spring. We find them but it's no good, never mind it was worth a try. We drive down to a lake , it's beautiful and free parking, perfect , but thousands of mosquitos!!

Monday 31st May 2010.

Off to Narva, the border town, we are going to clean ourselves up, ready for Russia. We have found the Hotel Narva, great it's just five minutes from the border crossing. We took a stroll up and saw the cars queuing to cross. There is also an enormous castle by the river, it's great for photos, but I've left the camera in the hotel!!!

Went and had a pizza then a beer in the hotel room and we found an English channel on the television, such a treat. It was showing a film that we had not seen before.

Wow---Russia tomorrow!!!!!!!!!!!!!!!!!!!!!!!!!!!!!!!!! Can hardly believe that I have just written that. Russia, even the name is intimidating to me, I have visions of scenes from unnerving films...............!! Stop it!

Tuesday 1st June 2010

Forgot to mention yesterday that Darren managed to get the spring welded, the trailer is now all fixed, it's as good as new!!!.......Off to Russia today, hoping for a pleasant surprise. We need to get car insurance and some cash, we have read that you can buy insurance at the border, we'll soon find out!

Arriving at the crossing we join the queue of cars. There are only about ten cars in front of us. Sitting and waiting, we decide it would be a good idea if I went to the guards office and ask about the insurance. I arrive and, in my best English, while nervously smiling, ask the guard my question. He answers, "No, go transit place" and he pointed at a map, well, he understood me. O.K ....several kilometres up the road, at the "transit place" I leave Beverley and Darren in the car, and walk over to what is a dreadfully decaying bunch of portable offices. I warily enter , one door leads to a corridor to another door, here there is a window in the wall, behind which is a woman. She listens to my attempts to explain why I am here and replies "no insurance here--buy at border--20 euros please for ticket for border queue"...O.K.. so I pay, without protest, and retrace my steps, very thankful to be back outside.

At 11.30am we joined the queue again . I give the guard the ticket, we will never know if such a ticket is actually needed. I again asked for insurance, his reply "I know not this word insurance," strange, he knew the word earlier this morning!!

1pm...through the first barrier and told to wait. We are asked for the papers for the trailer, but we don't have any. It's an old 1968 trailer, we believed that no papers were needed, well not in Europe, Darren does his best to explain this.

1.10pm they said ok, and sent us to next queue.

1.30pm haven't moved an inch....

2.05 moved a few feet through a red light and given custom and migration papers to fill in...

2.20 still queuing...

3pm same....

3.30pm moved a bit and handed in papers...they told us we had filled them in wrong and to do it again, we do, but they are still wrong , we do it again and make copies, as instructed. Then we are asked for the papers for the trailer. Darren explained it all again.

4pm...Refused entry and told to wait. All the guards have guns, they look at us and point. One walks around us with a huge dog. I can understand we need checking, but they are making me feel guilty, for what?

5pm still waiting. .(bladders bursting, the toilet facilities are indescribable)....

6pm still waiting--- they keep looking at us, do they want a bribe? Darren has tried to give them an excuse to take some cash from us, by asking if we can pay for the necessary documents, we are sure this is what they want, ...

7pm Entry refused, because of trailer, we are sent back to Estonia. We go straight back to the Hotel, and the toilet. We cancelled the bank card before we left, will it work, fingers crossed.   Yes, the card is still working, so at least we are safe for tonight.

We decide that, if we want to continue with the journey, the trailer will have to go. We will not give up. Speaking to the lady at the hotel reception, she told us she knew somebody who worked for a charity, helping homeless people, and thought the trailer may be of use to them, so it is arranged that the trailer will be collected in the morning. We start sorting out what we have, an awful lot of food, pasta, beans, flour. Darren stops people who are walking by and gives them bags of food, soon we have a crowd of about thirty people, word spreads quickly. I have books, and private things I have kept, to remember our previous life. I have to decide, quickly, on the spot, what to keep, what to pass on. There is only a small space in the Landy to re-house these items, along with packing as much food as is possible.   I find this very emotional, out with the tissues, again. I have such mixed feelings, I love giving things away, I want to keep more than is possible, although I'm sure we can live without most of it, and we're going to Russia tomorrow. I feel that we are leaving half our worldly goods in Estonia, well we are - - do I laugh or cry. I don't actually have a choice it's both!

Then we had pizza and went to bed.....what a day!!!!!!!

Wednesday 2nd June

Terrific storm last night, I hope the tents have stayed dry!!....

11am, and as agreed our man came for the trailer, we followed him and dropped it off at a garage. We say our goodbyes and give our trailer away, all sorted, perhaps it will do some good work for the charity.

We are a bit squashed in the car, but hey, it doesn't matter...but all that work, time, money, food, effort, and memories--- gone--just like that.!!!!

We buy another ticket for the queue, we are at the border and ready to try again....

12.10pm back in queue.....

2.30 in Russia. They checked our passports and paperwork, time and time again, all this paperwork is crazy, we have paid for what might be insurance. All done now, perhaps if we had done a little more research we might still have the trailer, but it's easy to say that, after the event. Maybe it will be easier to travel without it.

5.10pm St. Petersburg --the car in front is a ford focus called a Rolf!!....8.50 still driving around looking for hotel. The traffic is unbelievable, it's taken us hours to move just 5km. Cars driving on pavements to overtake and pushing into queues, every driver thinks that they are the only important one on the road. We put music on, David Bowie, that's better, now it becomes fun again. People are waving and taking photos of us, we manage to move some more. We are getting nowhere, so we stop to buy a satnav!!! St. Petersburg is a beautiful city. It's very hard work for us, as strangers, but well worth the visit!!

10pm. We have found a motel, but no cash point. So we just take one room and bring in the sleeping bags. We can now stretch our legs out for a bit, there is zero leg room in the car!!!

Thursday 3rd June

9.30 back on road heading for Moscow, it's dull and cloudy but not cold. Looking for a shopping centre for a cash point. Yesterday we took out 2000 rubels, but it converted to only about £40 so we need more.

Arrived in Novgovrod about 12pm. Stopped by the police. Darren knew they were asking for papers but he pretended he didn't understand and just spoke in English. They waved us away, the question is - do we have insurance???

There is one straight road from St. Petersburg to Moscow. It's full of lorries, of all shapes and sizes, some are just enormous, they swerve around the pot-holes from one side of the road to the other in a zig-zag. The houses along the side all seem to be of the same design, just different colours, pink and green or blue, green and purple!!!!

We have attempted to stop a couple of times but keep finding horseflies. We know that Darren has an allergic reaction to them and that's the last thing we need, so 7pm looking for hotel/motel. Diesel is now 40pence per litre..

Friday 4th June

Woke to a big storm in a motel 150 km short of Moscow. It's hot and clammy today.

Arriving at Moscow (MOCKBA) 11.50am...8 lanes of traffic with zebra crossings--people just walk out, some don't even look!! Still arriving at 12.50. At 2.20pm still driving round. Eventually we found a hotel, but no thank you , there are armed guards at all the doors, don't like the look of it.

5.15 still driving, but now leaving Moscow. We had wanted a few days in a hotel and time to wander around the city, but it's just impossible. Never again will we visit Moscow it's the worst city we have ever been in, with the worst drivers and the worst road system (wouldn't mind flying in and visiting 5 star with all the touring organised). We have seen a good ten accidents today, they just seem to swerve into each other, then everyone stops to wait for the police. It's no wonder they don't like trailers. Eventually we find a pitch, off road, with no horse flies, and it's quiet!

Saturday 5th June

 Darren has checked the car and found what the noise is, it's the rear prop shaft, so he has removed it to sort it out when we are in a better place.

We set off on the motorway and there was, what I thought,   a very loud bang, it really scared me. Darren calmly drives to the side of the road and stops - the hand brake drum has fallen off.   It could have caused a nasty accident, we were lucky! Darren reclaims it from the middle of the road, something else to fix!! We parked up and Darren fixed everything!!...then we drove off road, behind some trees, and found a beautiful meadow without mosies ---perfect...........

Sunday 6th June

A lovely sunny day—we are heading south for Tyna. We did the washing at a standpipe and put the rubbish into the burning bin at the side of the road, seems normal to burn the rubbish this way, the fire smoulders away as people keep adding to it, and why not--it works, bit smelly though!!.....We got stopped by the police again, this time they asked us where we are going, took a photo and let us go. There is a petrol station every 300--to 500 metres, we had heard it might be hard to find fuel??---Now we are heading for Bopohex---found another lovely field to camp in..... today is my Birthday, it's brilliant!

Monday 7th June

9.50--29 degrees---Bopohex is a good-looking, very clean city, and we are enjoying the journey again now we are out of the major traffic in Moscow. We also did a bit of shopping and bought Beverley a leather jacket, just what she had been looking for.

Off towards a lake or maybe the black sea. Looking at the map I can't tell if the two join together. Found a beautiful camping spot in a meadow, the colours of the flowers are striking.

Tuesday 8th June

We found the lake, the water has that sulphur smell, and thick black sticky sludge in the bottom. We are sharing our camp site with a herd of cows, therefore, we have named this spot 'cow-pat beach,' exceptionally whiffy and squelchy but that's nature!!!

Wednesday 9th June

We drove and saw a grey haired, bearded man on a pushbike. He was obviously a traveller, Darren slowed down, and as we approached called "hello, can you speak English?"   "Yes of course" came the reply, sounding almost offended to be asked such a question. His name is Ivan, and he comes from the Isle of Man... (which the flag on the back of his bike obviously denoted – whoops). We stopped for cups of tea....Ivan is doing the same trip as us---all alone on his pushbike--now that's what you call brave (or mad). He is a fascinating chap, could have spent hours talking with him.

Later we stopped to replenish our water tank, at a well, at the side of road in a village. An elderly lady came out to greet us, she seemed absolutely convinced that we could understand every Russian word she spoke. We could understand that she was overjoyed to be talking with us, and then she insisted on giving us a bag of fish, the bag felt warm, then as it got hotter I realised it must of been in the process of being smoked. Such kindness, but we have stopped eating meat and fish, and none of us can face it, so we gave it to the local cats!!

 Just outside the village we saw a graveyard, it was full of blue painted tables and benches. Further on, the road is lined with olive trees. We are directed to the dirt tracks, we reflect on the possibility of a satnav having a nervous breakdown.

3.30 arrived in Enck, it's a seaside town with people windsurfing, and a pleasant beach. We took a swim, refreshing. Here, there are many bars, and lots of the usual junk for sale, and plenty of entertainment for young children. Beautiful fragrant roses and poppies are everywhere--- is this the same country??? We set up camp on a quiet beach, me and Beverley did our best to ignore the smell. We are all tired and don't want to move, but it really should of been named 'Dead Fish Cove'. We drove up onto the cliff top---to the annoyance of Darren, who has no sense of smell (lucky thing)--later to be known as 'Insect cliff '!!! Happy birthday Darren.......

Thursday 10th June

It is awfully hot and smelly, we are bitten, itchy, spotty, with plenty of sore bits, but we are all fine. We saw Ivan again and stopped for tea (of course), I made Ivan a cheese and Branston pickle sandwich, he gave us a bag of cherries.

We are heading for the coast of the Black Sea, we can see nowhere to stop, it's all rice fields and mosquito's. We drove through a village, there were no satellite dishes, that's unusual. Then we get stopped by police for crossing a white line, about a tyre width, out comes the gun, they threaten us with pay now or they will take Darrens' driving licence-- fined 200 euros, Luckily we had enough money but now down to last 100 euros emergency fine money!!! Found a parking spot, but we are not hidden from the road, its 8.30pm and we've all had enough, Darren is so tired!! All that time wasted with the police!!!! A moped comes and checks us out three times, and then a car, a couple of times, now Russia is really scaring me. Thoughts of how we could just disappear off the face of the earth!!!! Darren goes and sits in the car for hours, allowing us to sleep in the roof tent, well, that was the idea, not a good ovoningll

Friday 11th June

Nothing happened last night!!! I'm sure that it was because Darren was watching, a few vehicles came, but they could see he was guarding us, and left, phew!

It's 9am, nobody is up, except me. I am waiting for a lorry to move on, so I can go to the toilet! Eventually he moves off and I dive behind a tree!

We all wash our hair with the rest of the water, from our water tank. A very drunk man arrives on a moped, again convinced we can understand his every word. We pack up and move on.

Drove to AHANA, it's a very busy, typical seaside resort. We see the black sea, it's gorgeous. We drive down the coast to find a pitch, if we can, found some water and a cash point, which is always a relief! Appears to be a wealthy place---lots of vineyards, never thought of Russian wine, we must try some. We saw people carrying beach towels, so we parked and followed them, they lead us to a beach where we swim, with masses of jelly fish. Beverley was a little nervous of the jelly fish at first , but soon got the knack of putting them on my head and down the front, and back, of my swimming costume. We drove on--nowhere to stop....Hot Hot...we drove up a dry mountain track—it looked just like Spain----camped—brilliant, just us here!!!!

Saturday 12th June

Drove down the coast road and we spotted a campsite. It's on the beach, this is fun, we go for a swim the water is warm, beautiful. Is this really Russia? It's hot, hot, hot!

Only one thing which spoils it and that's the toilet block. I started heaving at a distance of about 50 foot. There are no doors on the cubicles and nobody uses toilet paper, well, I shall be doing a lot more swimming!!!!!!!

Sunday

We stay on the campsite and swim in the sea......

Monday

Stayed again--- While I am swimming, Darren decides to check the car out, he comes from underneath and catches his head on the door , blood pouring, Beverley comes

to find me, I am on my way back, it was a close thing---just short of a hospital job!!!----After a while we went to walk to the cash point , it's very hot—really too hot to go walking. Something made me look down at my hands, and my fingers had changed into big fat sausages. I don't know why, must be the heat, it's a bit frightening, so I lifted my hands up and kept moving my fingers??? Well I'm still alive!!! Back at the campsite we met a Russian family and drank tea with them. They've invited us to their house tomorrow evening, will meet at 6pm.

Tuesday 15th June

Stayed at the camp again to meet up with the Russian couple, but they had disappeared. We drove back to the mountain where we had camped on Friday, as it was too late to find new pitch. We had another huge thunderstorm, had to sit it out in the car—un-nerving!!

Wednesday 16th June

Set out for Caspian sea---east---straight across.   We camped in a field, glanced at the time, 7pm. That's when we realised we had missed a time zone, yesterday we went to meet, our new friends, the Russian couple, an hour late. Although, they would of had to drive past us to leave, oh well, perhaps they had second thoughts, we will never know!

Thursday 17th June

Hot hot .....we all got chewed by mosies last night, the noise of the crickets is drowning out our radio . We are driving S.E., about level with South of France or Italy.

We were stopped by the police again, I confess I thought, 'here we go again', but money was not the reason, he sent us another way up the motorway because of trouble in Chechnya, which we were, apparently, heading for.

We have been stopped seven more times. Some police had guns, which they pointed at Darren as they took him to their car. We could hear shouting, then, Darren shouting back at them, they wanted money, but Darren has had enough. He insists that they take him and make it official, in the end they give up. It terrified me. This happens a few more times, I can't help thinking that I want to go home, but, I am home, this is where we live, in James the Landy !!

After forcing a few positive thoughts into my mind, about what an experience this is, and how hard we have all worked to get here, things start to feel better. The last stop today, and the police were just curious, seeing a zebra car driving towards them, we do ask for it, as we drove away, they gave us a salami sausage

6.45pm and the desert has started, we make camp and see a huge spider, giant millipede, crickets, locusts, and dung beetles, the latter being brilliant -- as soon as you have finished going to the toilet they are there, and it all disappears in minutes !!!!!

Friday 18th June

We think our Russian satnav really is having a breakdown--we set the route, but before we have even moved it is saying "you have left the route". We set off 10.20am , it is hot and a little rainy, Diesel is now 25p per litre. 1.30pm we are stopped by police again, all ok.

We have noticed that peoples' faces are now appearing to be more Asian. The main road is now a sand desert track. Beverley notices that there are sea shells everywhere, was the Black sea and Caspian, once one big sea? There are pink and yellow flowers spread around, and its hot. After talking about it for quite a while, we have decided, that in our experience, the Russian people seem to be not very happy !!! 4pm another police stop all ok ---camped in dung beetle field....

Saturday 19th June

The road is brown because it is densely covered in large crickets, as we drive there is a crunching sound, the air is thick with them, they climb all over the front bonnet and windscreen wipers, it's very hot, but our windows remain closed!

Peoples' faces are now looking oriental. We stopped at a shop, they are very friendly. Now we have 22km of grit and sand road. The police stopped us and asked to see our insurance papers--we showed them the tickets we were given, but no good, we had paid for insurance but not given any, as we thought. They asked where we are going, when we said we were heading for the border they just told us to go!! This was brilliant, we give the police a really good reason to book us, and these turn out to be friendly, it's a funny old world!

  Arrived at a town and drove round and round, the satnav has definitely lost it, so frustrating. We found a place to camp only to be eaten by midges, they fly into your face --into your eyes, up your nose and in your ears...yuk, Eventually the midges go to bed, and so do we.

Sunday 20th June

Off to the border, we are all prepared and ready to cross tomorrow. Beverley is listening to music, Darren is playing bogle on the nintendo...It's so hot - 35 in the shade,.We have managed to buy some bread and found a good water supply at a standpipe.......camped..

Monday 21st June

We have had a good night --not too many bites, which is good because we have dozens already.

 The visas for Kazakhstan start today, so off we go........our 18th country, and it's a hot 45 degrees. We crossed a river on a very iffy bridge, it creaked loudly, we knew it was safe only when we got to the other side. Then we saw a herd of horses running free, it's a sight that is so beautiful and exciting it takes your breath away. I felt so fortunate and in such high spirits, watching the young foals leaping, the wind blowing in their manes, wow,   creaky bridges are nothing !!!

At 11am we arrived   at the Russian customs and handed in all our papers. They did not check anything. that we were made to declare, on entering Russia. Next passport control and it was o.k.---2 hours and we are through. There is then 10km of no-mans land leading to the Kazakhstan customs.

We arrive and they split us up. Darren is sent to drive through with the car, while me and Beverley go into the customs building to find passport control. I don't like this, we feel very vulnerable without Darren. After a long wait, we are through and meet up again. Now Darren is sent off to passport control, while we wait in the car. We waited and waited.

An elderly lady, in the car parked next to us, keeps wailing. We can't understand what she is shouting and why is she there. I would like to go and offer her some help, but to be quite honest I am afraid to get involved, not very proud of myself. After a while some people get into the car with her, now she appears to be happy. Maybe I was wise to stay away, I like to think so anyway.

After another twenty minutes Darren comes back, he needs 500 rubels for the customs man, 'special price for tourists' - 50 rubels for anyone else!!!

It's 2.30pm and Darren still has to sort out insurance, well at least we may get some this time. He returns and then all we need is a few bribes. We reluctantly give them our walkie talkies and a knife and a pen they took a liking to, they want more and more but we have to say no. Luckily they seem satisfied with their gifts and agree to let us pass, phew!

At 3pm we enter Kazakhstan......   We see more wild horses, beautiful. The houses are made of wood, with flat roofs, so we guess there is not much rain here. We see graves everywhere. Beverley says "Is it me, or are they camels over there?" She is spot on, they are everywhere!!! ....

We pitched up on a flat sandy area, and cooked rice, we can see just one house in the distance. A shepherd comes to say hello, we communicate in gestures. He stays and eats with us, he invites us to go sleep at his house, we decline and thank him. He fetches his neighbour and we drink water together, the shepherd tells us he has 400 sheep........ what a fantastic experience........

Tuesday 22nd June It's very windy.... heaps to see today, camels, horses, goats, graves. We saw a house standing alone, just one house, nothing else, bit too much of a quiet location!! Stopped at an oasis, not a pretty one, but its water we can use,, me and Beverley had a paddle and we did the washing.

Me and Beverley are dreaming of a hotel again--no shower or bath since 3rd June--plenty of buckets but it's not quite the same. We did have a portable shower, but that had to go with the trailer, there was no space for it.

We are soon to arrive in Actipay, our first big Kazakhstan town. It's near the Caspian sea, which up to now, has been a big, big disappointment, so we are not holding our breath!!

Well it turns out to be a huge modern city, with a better feel than the Russian cities, the people just seem to be much happier, and we have heard some English being spoken. Again people have the right of way and just walk out into the traffic. We are trying to find a map, so we ask at a garage, no good. Two young men offer to show us the way to a shop where we can buy one. Their names are Cherub and Fernando, after following them from shop to shop we are then passed over to their friend whom we follow for a while. Between them all, they cannot find us a map or a compass or a satnav!!! They are just so helpful and smiley, we are told that a friend of theirs will have a map for us, he is about 100km further on our route........

We drive on through the town and camp in the desert, it's good , just a few mosies.........

Wednesday 23rd June.

It's cooler today only 35 in shade....off up north to Actobe today. There is a long and a short road, we opt for the short. The long is supposed to be quicker because of the better road surface, but we reckon James is up to it, and it should be more fun......We come to a salt lake which still has some water in it. We have seen many white, long dried out salt flats. As we walk down to it our feet sink into the oil in the ground and it sticks to our shoes.

Moving on, and I think the sun has got to me because, for some reason, I try to read the road sign backwards, as if reading Russian isn't difficult enough, backwards is ridiculous We follow the track, we have only a tiny map of Kazakhstan, in our Russian map book. No compass, as that decided to jump out of the window off the dashboard, luckily we still have Sandy the satnav, she has no idea where she is, but can tell us north or south. We go off the so called road, and onto the mud track, that runs alongside, it is better.   Now we have a hundred miles of bone shaking track.. We see our first prairie dog (aah! sweet just like a big gerbil). We see horses, they are sheltering in huge drainage pipes. It's 48 degrees in shade......We stop to camp but we were too near the road, or really too near a track, which turns out to be in use. So we try to move, but can't start, the starter motor is dead!!! A lorry came along and they kindly pull started us, now we have to camp on a hill, so we can roll start in the morning.

Thursday 24th June

We spend the night parked on a hill, trying not to roll out of our tents, it works, the downhill start is successful...We passed watering holes and saw some gargantuan vultures, fantastic. The road is a white knuckle ride that lasts for hours, there is dust and dust!!! We see herds of animals in the distance -- this is how I had imagined Africa to look, out of this world, the sand is sucked up into big twisters, some completely engulf the car. We stop at a town to fill up with water and buy bread; the people are so very friendly.   Darren is given a bottle full of milk and told to leave it in the sun for two days--this is the famous fermented mares' milk that we thought was only in Mongolia!!! It's hot, 46 degrees in shade...

.9.15 pm now 30 degrees---hoping to get a starter motor tomorrow, there are better ways of camping than pitching up on a hill, tonight it is very steep, hope we don't slide out of bed!!!!

Friday 25th June

It's 7am and already 30 degrees in the shade, the roll start worked again.

11.30am the police stop us--all ok. At 11.45am the police stop us again, this time they want money. They accused Darren of being a drunk driver, they made him roll up our insurance papers and blow through them--said they could smell vodka, then they asked for money. These tactics seem to be well practised, and maybe they work well, but not with us!! Darren said "No - -we have no money-"- they don't like this, so they try to get me to admit Darren had been drinking, and then accused Beverley of drinking.....very scary!! Darren held his ground and said a firm " NO, " then they just gave him the papers back and let us go. It doesn't do me any good thinking about what could have happened, nobody knows where we are, we could just disappear of the face of the earth. Should we be here, well we are, by our choice, time to start thinking positive.

We arrived at Aktobe at 12.30pm, it's a huge city. Apparently it started off as a Russian fort, and it has a fantastic mix of old and new. Old soaring mosques and churches, alongside modern tower blocks. We found a garage where they say they can fix the starter motor, but they want £450 , good day for the garage, we have no choice. At 3.15 we are still waiting. It is so hot, very hot, 43 degrees in shade—we are so glad we have our fridge!!! Poor Beverley has a really bad stomach today, with a lot of discomfort. The only toilet belongs to the garage, which is best not described, I'll just say that the plumbing was missing, hygiene didn't come into it, and the smell <><>< not where you want to be when your ill, poor Beverley!

Another hour passes and the work is finished, but surprise, surprise, the price has gone up, we explain we have no more money, we cannot take anymore out of the cash point – even if we wanted to. After some intorooting dehating, the garage owner understands that he cannot extract any more cash from us, all is ok, we can leave.

At 5.30pm we are looking for a hotel, and we found one straight away---the Hotel Daston Aktobe, it even has pizza on the menu ---shower bath and wifi !!!

Saturday 26th June

There is only one problem with the hotel, the mosies come in through the vents, so we have a new consignment of bites---could be worse. After a good sleep, food and a shower Beverley is much better, she's a very strong person, good job she is!!!!

Off to Aral and the Aral sea. It's 46 degrees in the shade, we are not too sure of the way, without a map. There is a definite lack of sign posts, we think we are off route and retrace our way by 60 miles---camped for night--no mosies!!!

Sunday 27th June

It's 50 degrees in the shade, it may be higher, it's gone off the scale!!!! Darren gave James a check-up---the back end of the chassis is broken and the roof is lifting above the windscreen, All together a sorry sight, the oil is leaking out of the transfer box at the rate of about 1 and a half litres per week-----will James survive??

At 4pm we saw our first proper oasis -- not with actual palm trees, but some sort of trees. and one lone house, what a place to live. We drive on into more desert, and more desert, we camped --watched the most glorious sunset—then went to bed.

Monday 28th June

A good night, and at 11am and we are on the road, it's 37 degrees in the shade. We drive through the seemingly endless desert. Darren is well practised with the speed he has to drive at to cope with the corrugated roads, but even so they are shaking and rattling poor James, and us.

 I have learnt to make sandwiches in the back of the car, it is quite an art to prepare food when it is jumping in the air, it's amazing what you can do!

Heading S.E. we stop for water at a small town and started talking to the locals. They ask us to stay, we have tea with bread and jam. They are so friendly and just want to share everything they have with us. The mother, Lisa, invited us to stop the night and to have a shower, it's tempting, but we decide to move on. Inside the cool, mud brick, house they have everything, including a microwave oven and satellite t.v., of course. Lisa asked us to come back again so she could cook us a big meal with all her family, as we left she gave us a homemade loaf and took photos .Lovely people, we will remember them.

We drove on a while, we see huge birds of prey..... then we stopped to watch the wild horses -- unbelievable-- what a day. We stopped for supplies, but they had no diesel. After 101 miles we have had enough, after being rattled to pieces. There is enough diesel for 60 miles and it's about 35 miles to the next town, fingers crossed.

We camped and see that there were prairie dog holes everywhere. Darren killed a fly with his hand then wiped his hand with a tissue to remove tiny maggots Yuk yuk!! ! There is absolute silence here -- no birds no crickets, just the odd fly which I believe belong to the prarie dogs, who are hiding, but we cannot stop here as the flies are biting Darren, so we move on a mile or so,and it's all ok.......

Tuesday 29th June

Another 30 miles of dust road—we came to a junction, as we had hoped, found diesel and filled up the tank for about £22, as it was only 33pence a litre.

Now going south east towards the Aral sea, on a tarmac road, well for 5 miles anyway. Then it's back to sand and gravel with huge potholes, and chunks of road just missing. The road is blocked off for repairs, again--in places there are thousands of pounds worth of machinery, but you never see anyone doing anything, no matter what the time of day.

I have got my lap seat belt on tight - it stops me from banging my head on the roof---the car is full of dust, lots of twisters today. Suddenly we see what looks like a huge lake, but it's a mirage---the temperature has gone off the scale it is 55 degrees plus!! As we pass lorries we get engulfed with dust and can't see anything for a few seconds---eventually 3pm a bit of not too bad road----and a sign Aral 116km

Arrived, it's a huge place, but not modern at all, except for the town square which stands alone with it's statues. The rubbish is dumped everywhere, there are slums, or should I say poor areas, all around and numerous strolling cows. We find a tiny shop, a young girl- maybe 16 - speaks to us in English, we ask her where the sea is, but she has no idea, and neither has anyone else they just say it's a long way. We go back to the desert to camp for the night....

Wednesday June 30th

Off to find the Aral sea, it must be somewhere. It's a hot one today, 60 degrees in the sun. After hours of being shaken silly in the car, we come across the famous ships in the desert. You can still tell that they were once ships, but now are just huge chunks of rusty metal, abandoned as the sea receded. Now they are bringing shade to several camels, the other ships of the desert, haha. Then we drive another 5 and half miles to reach the sea. The beach is softer than we thought, we sink into it. Eventually we dig ourselves out, having to use the four sand boards--- without them I don't think we would have been able to get out. As we were digging, the holes were filling with sea water. I was not happy, my head full of frightening thoughts. Darren was his usual calm self, and in the end we won, just as he said we would.

Driving back we stop to collect a few shells and Beverley takes a photo of a fish in a bush, how it got there we do not know. It is 8 and a half mile drive to the village, which used to be on the water's edge. Darren is exhausted now, he had no sleep last night with his bad knee. We stopped for the night -- Darren mended the wiring and then changed a UJ- what an incredible mechanic he is. We put the tents up--no flies tonight!!!!

Thursday July 1st

Back to Aral for supplies...At the watering well, a local lady gives us one of her water bottles, she warns us that in the next few days there is going to be a heatwave of 70 plus. We decide to head up to Astana, the capital in the north, but it will probably take us at least 3 days. It is so hot that fresh bread is crispy before you can finish making a sandwich, and if you put a bottle of water in the front of the landy for a while it is hot enough to make a cup of tea. The metal parts in the car burn to the touch, there is no shade anywhere, we haven't seen a tree for ages....this is good training for the Gobi !!!!

Friday 2nd July

10am hot. Last night, we were all bitten heaps of times, there were thousands of tiny mossies, they were so small they were getting in through the nets. Hopefully it seems that we haven't got any bad reactions.

11am the landscape is changing again, it's now green and swampy, agricultural and pongy!!!   We are now heading for the town of Kizylorda. Getting closer to the town we see a sheltered bus stop full of horses , it's the only shade. We found the bizarre and bought a new grease gun (we drove over the other one), We also found pop and juice and samosas---Darrens' face when he tasted the samosa—yum, tasty food!

1pm now heading back N.E. it's gone deserty again---at 3.50pm the milage reads 149325 we have driven exactly 10,000 miles !!!!! The roads gone very bad again bumping and banging us around, then the car sets on fire-- we all jumped out-- it was the battery..all ok. That's what you get if you shake a car battery very hard !!!!!

Saturday 3rd July

The mileage now reads 149353.... Following the battery incident , Darren does all the repairs - all is fine. It's a good job he is so competent as the nearest town, or village, is around 100 miles either way. We camped in the desert--no mosies, but terrific winds, we hardly slept, then it started to rain. If this is a biggy it's possible that the ground could change to mud, so we got on the move quickly. Beverley said she was cold, although the temperature still reads 27. Two hours and still raining, white and pink flowers are blooming, changing the landscape, beautiful. We arrived at a large town and the people are European looking. We have to admit we are lost!!! We ask many people, and have lots of photos taken, but nobody can tell us the way. Eventually after several attempts we found our way out to the North, to the capital.

The earth changes colour to a bright red, after a few miles bright orange, then normal sandy colour;, then the colour is green----green sand and rocks, it's amazing!

We start to make camp, a man on a horse appears and seems to indicate something about sacred ground, he rides off. We make tea and wait, we have a feeling that someone will arrive. Soon a car appears, a man steps out, he is very friendly and invites us to his house for tea, ok, we follow him, it's about ten minutes to the village. He is the mayor of the town, he gives us a beautiful book, which is partly written in English. We had understood the man on the horse, yes, the ground is sacred. The mayors wife offers us tea with bread, jam, biscuits, cream, sweets and salty meat - mutton I think. Then all this is followed by a very large dish of fermented mares milk - served cold. I cannot describe the taste to be like anything, it's drinkable, but it will not become one of our chosen drinks. Darren drank it too and he hasn't touched milk in over twenty years. They asked us to stay the night and offered us more mares milk and vodka, very kind, but at this point we decided it was probably best to leave.-They gave Beverley a leather computer bag with a diary and boxed pen -- lovely gift...

Monday July 5th

149744......I did repairs on the tents, bits of sewing etc., - Beverley drives the first ten miles this morning, through the fields, she is very good!! The land is completely flat. There are fields of wheat, and hay, miles long and miles wide, hay cutting is going on all over the place, Hot today 40 degrees in the car.....the roads are so bad we are driving on small tracks using the satnav as a compass. 12.30pm Beverley takes the wheel for another half hour. 1.30 and we run out of tracks ending in an empty derelict village--deserted--we see a lovely watering hole but as we approach it is all dung and mud! After backtracking a bit, and trying another track, we eventually end up at the main road. Almost a motorway, well two- way traffic, on tarmac, this lasts for 100 miles then back to potholes........

Tuesday July 6th

149933......We discover that we had cut off a corner by going across the fields. Now we are soon to arrive in the capital Actaha--in English Astana. The temperature has dropped, it's still hot and sunny, the land is green, with trees, we have not seen a tree for ages. We arrive, and there is a car broken down in the middle lane, Darren stops and gives him a tow.

 Now to find a hotel. The first we find is 5 star - £500 a night each, they kindly give us directions to hotel number 2.   4 star - £150 a night for all of us -- we decide it's still too much for a few days, off to hotel number 3 ---what's a star???? -- £70 a night for all three of us, breakfast included, we book two nights. It's a very large room with three clean, large beds tv, and a bath, luxury!

Wednesday 7th July

We have spent the day shopping, bought a new horn for James as he sounds more like a mouse than a Landrover. We have an internet connection and spend the evening talking to Didier, in France, and catching up.

Thursday 8th July

Sightseeing===Palace of peace and accord----brilliant building in the shape of a pyramid. The lifts have to go sideways to fit into shape— cool. We all love Astana it's a beautiful city, with many stunning buildings and gorgeous gardens. We also visit the tower and are rewarded with striking views across the city, you can see the edge of the city as it changes into the desert.

Friday 9th July

150078.... We prepare to leave for Almaty. At 3.30pm we are off, we see a sign it says Almaty 1165km... on our map that's about 3 inches!!

Saturday 10th July

150145. A good night. .Off for 10.30am, the temperature has dropped, it's now quite cool.

Sunday 11th July

150313. It's a bit cold. Back to salt flats and camels...drove down to a lake, it's very touristy. Shame but just a bit too nippy for a dip. 2.30pm only 584km to go....

Monday 12th July

150585....272 miles yesterday........Not much sleep last night, there was a strong wind storm. 12.30pm we stopped to watch a herd of horses galloping freely, a stunning sight, and to be so close, it's awesome. 2pm stopped at a river for a paddle, the landscape is changing, there are trees both sides of the road and water everywhere, we see a canal and a lake. Then at 2.30pm with no warning - we see in the distance, right across our path, a snow topped mountain range, really strange to be so hot and to see all that snow.

100km to Almaty-----We arrive in the city and drive around for ages looking for a hotel, then at the traffic lights somebody in their car says hello and asks where we are from, we tell him and ask if he knows of a hotel, "Yes", he says, "follow me." After perhaps 10 minutes we arrive at the hotel Astra, our guide just waves and drives off! The hotel is fully booked except for single rooms, they say we can have three rooms, we ask to see one, it has a double bed and room for a sleeping bag on the floor, we tell them one room will be ok for us, at this they offer us a mattress and sheets. This is so generous of them, all for around £50 a night for all of us. To us the room is large, after the Landy, we are quite happy!!!!

Tuesday 13th July

We have a drive around, there are people everywhere hitching a ride, cars stopping all the time to give lifts, obviously the norm, the people seem happy, lots of smiling faces. We go for a walk around and buy a new horn for the Landy, (as the last one wasn't good enough) horns are used constantly like a second language, and as James is so large, we think he should have a voice to match.

Wednesday 14th July

Very hot, we spend the day walking around the town and finding markets. Almaty is another vibrant city with a mixture of new and old with the striking backdrop of the snow covered Tien Shan mountains.

Thursday July 15th

Very hot...Darren goes for a walk and finds a Landrover dealer. Later we go for a drive and the starter motor fails again, we get a tow start, and back to the Landrover dealer. Three weeks ago it cost us £600 to have the motor fixed, today it costs us £170 for a brand new one!! Back at the hotel we park the car in the shade to cool down, the sun is so hot the car is impossible to work on...later Darren takes off old starter motor.

Friday July 16th

150822.......Darren puts on new starter motor before it's too hot, and we prepare to leave the hotel. By 12pm we are on the road heading for a huge canyon we have been told about. I had left some apples, under cover, in the car, they are cooked right through!!

We start to drive up a mountain to visit a lake, but it's just too hot. James is suffering, the brake master cylinder has now gone, so it's back to Landrover dealer, but they have nothing. We drive back out the city and on, the landscape changes again. We camp on the side of a track, on both sides of us the bamboo must be ten foot tall, amazing!

Saturday July 17th

150916.......8.30am and it's 31 degrees in the shade!! We get fresh water from a well, nice and cold. Fresh bread, tomatoes, peaches, melon and apricots, a great breakfast. There are lots and lots of donkeys here, but not many horses......2pm we pass through a huge gorge, desert and mountains either side of us, it is so hot ,39 in the shade, and at least 69 outside, luckily we have cloud cover today!!! We enter the State National Park of Charin.

Sunday 18th July

151082.....yesterdays extreme heat turned into a storm -- no surprise there. We have had little sleep, again, and now we all have new sets of mosie bites. It's cooler now and as we drive in the rain through the mountains it reminds me of Wales......3pm the storm continues with rain and lightning, the Landy is leaking, Beverley and Darren have soaking wet feet and its dripping water through the roof!!!! We see a herd (if that's the right term) of camels perhaps 20 to 30 being rounded up by men on horseback.

Monday 19th July

151306.........Up at 5.30am because of the storm. A herd of cows pass us on both sides of the car, the bull comes and checks us out with a closer inspection. On the road for 7am - raining, but it soon clears. We go to see a lake it is massive, very beautiful. Stop and camp about 5pm, much cooler now, the sky is clear, crossed fingers for tonight we are all very tired!!!

Tuesday July 20th

151576....We all have a good nights sleep. Out on the desert floor, we see a strange insect, it is about 3" long and one and a half inches wide, it has the head of a locust, six legs, two which look like long spinnerets and it is grey, can't quite make it out!

By 12pm we are back on the road, we see an upturned trailer which was carrying water melons, most of which are now spread on the sand, we stop and check to see if the driver is there but there is no-one .On our left there is black sky and lightning - on our right a dead cow---pooh!!!! We are driving into the storm, then we see a van, off the road stuck in the sand/mud. Darren drives down to help them, and we also sink, we dig and drive ourselves out and get back on the road. Darren takes the sand boards down to them, they manage to escape, and are very grateful!!

We decide to drive away from the storm. After a few hours we are stopped by the police and asked for money,   they said we were speeding; (not an easy thing to do in James). Darren refuses to pay them and they ask for our camera,   Darren declines and they let us go........we arrive at Astana at 8.30pm and go to the same hotel as before.... the car insurance has now run out.!

Wednesday July 21st

151876 exactly 300 miles.......Last night, at the hotel, on our way to the Landy, to fetch our bags, we see Agnes and Alan walk in, with June and David. It is remarkable to think where we are, thousands of miles into our journey, and yet the world seems so small. We spend our time chatting and catching up, a wonderful evening had by all. It was very enjoyable to see Beverley and June chatting to each other, a lovely break for both of them.

This morning we walked to search out new car insurance, it cost us only £3 for ten days, and then we bought an even louder new horn for the Landy....lazy day!!!

Thursday July 22nd

Went for a good walk around the town, and passed through a beautiful park, then back to hotel and rested.....lazy day........

Friday July 23rd

Today we were chased by a car, it seemed that the young man just wanted to say hello, but as we drove off he followed us until we parked outside a shop. It turned out that his friends, who had shown us the way to Astana, had sent him a photo of us on his mobile phone, he showed it to us, absolutely delighted to have spotted us. Then more photos so that he could send them a photo back. .Later we had a couple of beers with Ian, a motorcyclist we met at the hotel, he told us about a few more buildings worth a visit....

Saturday July 24th

Off to visit Astana Tower, it has the most impressive views of the city, you can see right to the finish of the city -- there are no outskirts, no houses., just the start of the desert.....extraordinary. Then we went to a shopping centre which had a swimming pool on the top floor, a strange shaped building, it looked like it was falling over.

Darren fixed the Landy again, a policeman came over and told him to clean it......in the evening we watched Jackie Chan and then the Pirates of the Caribbean 2 .....in Russian or should I say Kazakhie??? It was very well dubbed and the voices were very well done.....

Sunday July 25th

151925....on road for 9am driving east to Pavlodar -- 250 miles --half way we stopped for supplies and topped up the phone. We drove up a path to camp for the night, screening ourselves behind some trees, Beverley found a cows foot -- lovely!!!

Monday 26th July

152156........After a good nights rest, we are driving N.E. It's 2.40pm and we are getting close to the last Kazakhstan town before the border!!! Ooh it's scary Russia next!!!!

We see huge fields full of sunflowers. We are heading for a storm. We arrived at the border named Kocok at 3.30pm and we managed to buy insurance!!!!

Feels a bit sad to leave Kazakhstan - we have driven over 5,000 miles here and it's been good.

It's 4pm and we are through the first barrier of the border, the car has been checked ---4.15pm second barrier and passports checked. Now to the Russian side------4.40pm 3rd barrier for passports....4.45 pm checked by dog at customs. 5pm through 4th barrier.... No problems, then at the final barrier, they sprayed our wheels with disinfectant, and then asked for 100 dollars to raise the barrier--- Darren was not amused - he told them "No money" ---they tried again ---"NO" -----OK, 5.05pm we passed through!!   Beverley comments that they are all like little Hitlers.

Almost immediately the landscape changes, it is much greener with many trees, it's raining with hefty black clouds!!!!.........5.45pm we stopped for a break, the mosies are enormous and we all get bitten again!!! 6.30 pm looking for a place to camp. Another time zone crossed and the hour has changed again, it is now 7.30.   We have a full phone signal, but the phone will not connect, it just gives us a message that we cannot read.

Tuesday 27th July

152322...The temperature is only 11 degrees....it's cold.   I was cold in the night, there are grey skies. We are on the road for 12.30pm...at 1.45pm we see the first police car, all ok, and they let us pass!!

 5pm and after a family discussion, we decide to change our plans, we were heading to lake Baikal, the worlds oldest and deepest freshwater lake,but it will mean travelling long distances for the next five days. We all feel that we would prefer to just leisurely drive straight down to Mongolia, through the mountains and enter on the west side. We have all seen many lakes, and feel that such an effort may end up with something we have said quite a few times before "Is that it?"

 We find a good pitch for the night, in a field behind a huge haystack, no mosies! We are just starting to watch a film, as it is dusk, and time for us to settle in. A farmer and his wife arrive to collect a horsecart full of hay. They welcome us, and let us know that they are happy with us camping here. We watch them loading the hay, and we say hello to the horse, it is fascinating to see the wooden tack that they use. It appears that things have not changed around here for countless years.

Wednesday 28th July

152525, On the road for 9am   .If this is summer in Siberia I can understand why husky dogs have such thick coats.

We see a genuine Russian cowboy, with a hat and a whip. There are huge tears in the earth where it has ripped open leaving mammoth gaping holes. Darren notices an interesting fact, that at least half of the cars are right hand drive. All the houses here are provided with underground hot water, and you can see the steam rising from holes in the streets.

We went into a town and bought a new phone card and Beverley found an Oggi shop, and bought another couple of outfits, she loves Oggi fashion, we first came across it in Astana, then Almati and now here in Russia.

Driving out of town looking for place to camp we find an empty hanger and decide to set up , it keeps most of the rain off us, enabling Darren to mend the headlights, which is good news as it is compulsory to have them on all day.   I was able to cook us all some hot food, it's only 15 degrees and very wet!!!!! The hanger has another room which appears to have an unpleasant amount of animal bones in it. Surrounding the hanger there are scores of sizeable plants which appear (from pictures I've seen), to be related to marijuana, does it grow wild here, hope we're not parked in somebody's secret garden.

Thursday 29th July

Arrive in BNNCK looking for jerry cans for diesel for Mongolia, we have no idea what it will be like for petrol stations, we have been told they can be hundreds of miles apart, we don't really believe that , but we have to be prepared, just in case.

As we drive on, we see a huge graveyard in the forest, not in a clearing, but in-between the trees, very unusual. As we head towards the mountains the plants are getting bigger, and taller, and the leaves are of titanic proportions. We then see a rope bridge made for cars, it looks extremely precarious, Darren and Beverley are ready to go, but, the car is too high, (thank heavens for that!).

We pitch in a lovely spot by the river, in a clearing just big enough to turn the Landy around.....

Friday 30th July

152806....lovely sunshine today and it's warm. We stopped at a shop for bread, and whatever we can find. They have no calculator, but an abacus, I never thought I would see one in use!

Getting higher now, 1590 and my ears can feel it!! We stop at a small town and walk around the market, I buy a warm jacket, and now I can throw away my old jumpers, which are so much trouble to wash and dry.

We see beautiful picture postcard villages, this area is stunning, it is called the Alty. We camp at a river, again. A car stops, a policeman steps out, he has run out of petrol, we give him what we have in our can , which we use for our cooker, he tells us this area has no trouble and we will be ok for another 100k. Then a family stop to say hello, the daughter speaks English, they say we are very brave. We light a fire and settle for the evening, cars and vans are passing, tooting horns and waving.......the people are much happier here!!!!!!

Saturday 31st July

152880,,,,,,,Beautiful day, have done all the washing in the river, workman stop in lorry to say hello, they are very friendly but as drunk as lords!!! We do our first river crossing, without any problems, and then stop for a picnic. The trees, mountains, it is all so WOW!!!!

Beverley has seen four white Siberian huskies so far, I have just seen my first--so gorgeous, we camp by the river again it's 35 in the shade.. happy. I never thought I would say this, but I really like this part of Russia.

Sunday 1st August......152958....Nice early morning cup of tea by campfire, followed by nice hot bath (in a tiny bowl but at least it's hot). We have all been bitten all over by mosies again--never mind could be worse!!! Stormy grey clouds today, as we sit there the cattle come over, one young bull tries several times to steal our clothes off the top of a bag, they are so cheeky, one empties our rubbish bag, we chase them off but they come straight back, they are very comically entertaining.

We are now just 70 miles from the Mongolian border. Beverley points out, what she calls a 'spine chilling sight', a dead carcass of a horse and about 20 large birds of prey!!!

The landscape has gone marshy now and we can see tons of snow on the mountains. Now there are huge flat plains of nothing, no crops, no animals. At every corner it changes.....it looks like the surface of the moon. Then it is so green, the sand and rocks all have a green colouration, I have never seen anything like this. The storm has gone now....next we are in a valley with a snaking river.

Now at 1800 metres.........3.15pm Kowaray, this is the last big town before the border. 50k to go before what is said to be the worse roads ever. James is being held together by 2 straps, poor thing, one to keep the roof on and the other to hold the chassis together, will he survive?

We meet a group of travellers going to China, and stop for a chat. Beverley spots our first big, hairy black cow, thick long black hair and a full tail, a yak, we think, beautiful!!

4.15 arrive at border...closed till tomorrow at 9am!!

Monday 2nd August.....153056...It was a rough night in the middle of an open plain (nowhere else to go) heavy rain and strong winds.....

We arrive at the border, there are lots of other travellers. Two friendly Swiss on pushbikes, Latvians, Russians and Lithuanians.

10.30 am passed through passport control. Then at customs we are asked for papers we do not have. We gave them the papers which we had been given in Kazakhstan. The papers were correct but they decided to make us wait anyway. Then it was the Landy to be searched—we opened up a tent , all ok...12.10pm and we are out.

Now 26k no-mans land to Mongolia......at the border we have no problems, they are about to close so we are rushed through. We exchange some money, a man in a grey suit asks for the papers for the car, he says that there is a big problem at customs and we must hand over all our papers and wait in the car. Darren has a feeling that this is just not right, he says " no thanks, we will drive back to the customs office and sort it out there". Darren had a hunch and he was right, needless to say nobody was there, the customs offices were all closed. We have possibly made a big mistake by changing too much money, we are annoyed with ourselves, but it's too late now. So we drive away, either people are trying to con us, or the police will follow us, we'll soon find out!

It's grey and cold and raining, with nasty bumpy tracks. Which way to go? There are no signs, then we see two land cruisers and decide to follow them.

Then a Kazakhstani man stops us, and asks us if we want a room for the night. He has all the questions he wants to ask us written on paper, he has worked at this. We are promised a hot shower and an internet connection. He wins all our votes for this , it's also Beverleys' nans birthday, it would be great if we could speak on skype.

 Off we go to see the room. What a lovely family, but the hot shower we were promised doesn't exist on the premises, just a short car ride, we decline the offer. The internet connection doesn't exist and the telephone line isn't real, it's an electric socket!, The room that they offered us consists of several beds/sofas, a cot, and other furniture.

We spend an hour or so with the family, they make tea and feed us a meal of sheep and potatoes, and they fetch us a couple of beers. They manage to find an extremely old and exceptionally expensive map, but they have to make a living. They have a baby, with no nappy, which the mother persistently places into Beverleys' arms, each time insisting a photograph be taken, poor Beverley!!!

Then the question of, where is the toilet? It is outside at the end of the front yard, next to the road. It is an open pit with a board to stand on, a three foot mud wall surrounds it with a wooden gate. As we approach the smell builds in strength. Darren is so lucky not to have any sense of smell! Well you could say it was sociable to be able to chat to passers-by whilst pooing, all good fun, if you can call it that, but not really our cup of tea. Darren, of course, finds this most amusing.

We have a kick around with the children and a football. An elderly gentleman, whom we assume is granddad, jokingly, we think, offers us money to sleep in our Landy, we decline the offer.

We have been thinking about our arrival, they seemed to know we were coming! Could it have been the man who stopped us at the border, did he phone ahead. It all feels somewhat uncomfortable. Other people arrive to stop in the next house, they are Russian, they speak a little English, we chat for a while. Feeling prickly about the whole situation, we decide it will be best to leave very early tomorrow.

So we spend our first night in a mud house with a flickering light bulb, in the most uncomfortable beds.

Tuesday 3rd August....up at 5am. The family run in and jump into the beds, it seems that they have been sleeping in their car and are nearly frozen. Now we understand the grandads offer! We move quickly and leave.

We follow the road out of town, there have been landslides, we manage to drive over the rocks and get through. We travel through a green river valley, there are many burial grounds and areas of animal slaughter where we see piles of goat and horses hooves.

After 60k we come to a deserted village--more burial grounds--and then the track ends at a derelict house. The ground ahead looks marshy, this is getting dangerous. We are trying to find the north road, but now it's snowing, and we are going nowhere, so we decide to head back to town. The views of the mountains, covered in snow are out of this world.

As we arrive back in town we see a man on a motorbike with a large live goat across his lap. We drive through, not seeing anyone from yesterday, phew! We leave the town again, this time, probably, heading on the south road, can't be sure, there are no signposts here!

We come across a man who is sitting at the side of the road with an enormous eagle that stands waist high, he wants us to take a photo for money, so we do, The bird is obviously so well trained, wow what a hunting tool.

Heading up towards snow covered mountains, through hail and snow, we come across a gigantic travellers truck, we stop for a chat, it is owned by a very amiable German man.

3.15pm ... 8000 ft on a dry, massive, flat, desert, plateau, with snow covered mountains both sides of us, sun shining on them. One looks just like a pyramid because the edges are so straight, it looks unreal. There are herds of horses, goats, long haired cattle and camels.

We drive through an icy river (while I hold my breath). Then we see the Mongolian tents - Gers- as we approach we are invited inside one for a cup of tea. It's made with milk and salt, they give us a taste of their cheese and biscuits, it's an experience but once is enough, I don't want to be ungrateful, and normally I can taste anything, but this cheese makes me want to vomit, it's so powerful. Inside the hut they hang dried meat, horse harnesses and all sorts, there are three tiny beds and a fire in the middle, they have a teeny tv run by a huge battery. It's warm, basic, has everything you need to survive (if your tough enough.).

We drive a little and camp by the side of a mountain--cold but dry---- 2000 metres high......

Wednesday 4th August.....153291......a good night--we have saved extra sleeping bags for Mongolia, so pleased we did! Stopped for a chat with group of Czech people driving two Ladas---drive a bit more and stop for another chat with some Czechs and a group of Germans in three big trucks. There is something special about meeting other travellers, always a pleasure.

3pm arrived at KHOVD-(-XOBA). The weather is lovely, we stop by a river and cook egg and chips and do all our washing. There are lots of people here, some having picnics, others washing carpets, horses and cattle wandering around. We see the two Ladas driving over the bridge and half an hour later the Germans pass, lots of tooting and waving!!!!

Mongolia is supposed to have the worst roads, but after Khazakstan it doesn't seem too bad at all, but maybe this is just the start?? Drive back out of town and camp with the mosies, we try and think of it as good practise for the tropics!!!

Thursday 5th August...153356..........Back into town for supplies, went to fill up with diesel but the pump was just pumping out vapour whilst measuring litres, we had to pay about £35 for next to nothing---luckily Darren spotted what was happening and stopped them, they were still asking for more money --Darren said "xxxx" and we drove away......

At the edge of the town we pick up Paul from Poland, he is hitchhiking, what a story, he tells us. He arrived with a couple of friends, they bought horses to travel this land, but disaster struck one night. They were camped by a river which burst its banks, the horses left and their bags were washed away, they thought they had lost everything. After a search they found some of their belongings. Pauls friends were able to leave, but Pauls' visa means he has to stay in Mongolia for another couple of months. Alone and broke, scary, but Paul just got on with it! When we prepare to camp, in our two very comfortable roof tents, we suggest he sleeps in the car, but he is quite happy outside, he has a bed roll and a mosquito net, this is all he wants.

We meet two French motorcyclists....we stop and chat.

There are dozens of spider crickets, just like the one we saw before, although these are only about 2 inches long they are still creepy, Paul picks one up and tells us they are harmless, that's good to know!!

Friday 6th August.......153481......we see herds of horses, they have very thick necks (one is lying dead at the side of the road), we learn that these horses are called Przewalski's horse, a very strong true breed, they need no help and feed themselves right through the winter.

After an hour on the road we see a Mongolian truck , broken down, the springs are broken. There are 6 people, and 1 ton of melons, which they are driving 1000k to sell, and we thought James was loaded! They have been here for 7 hours. Me and Beverley chat with the ladies, in sign language, they offer us cheese, we decline, I have learnt my lesson. After about half an hour, Darren and Paul get them moving again, slowly!!

1pm desert, no plants no animals nothing --- then some huts, how do these people live?? Arrived in town of Altay, Paul leaves us here to await the Germans he believes are going in his direction, we try to give him some money, just a bit so as not to offend him, but he won't have any of it. Good luck Paul.

Later we stop for water in a small village, it is very noticeable that a lot of the people are wearing nylon trousers and matching jackets, (now we know what happened to all the shell suits from the 1980's).....

We start to camp, two Austrian motorcyclists arrive and set up camp with us..........We have dreadful windstorms in the night, the tent is damaged, I think it can be fixed with a needle and some cotton.

Saturday 7th August......153637.........Miles and miles of open plains between the mountains...100k to a small town, in-between just the odd hut. There are sandy tracks to follow, but which one??? Most of them join up at some point, so we choose using the compass...

Yesterday we broke a teacup (small bowl) and as we drive Beverley spots one just sitting there all alone, strange! We stop and do repairs to the tents, a couple of horsemen come by with what looks like a dead beaver strapped to the saddle. It's very cold tonight, the grass is frozen and so is the flysheet.

Sunday 8th August......153749.........It's very green here, the road is corrugated with pot holes. We see lots of Mongolian cattle with long hairy coats and thick tails, we drive over shaky wooden bridges over very cold rivers. There are wild horses everywhere. The terrain changes to dry and sandy, and then there are acres of tiny purple daisies.

Looking at the map, the choices are north or south road? It seems we are already on the south road, as far as I can tell.

We camp by a river it's beautiful. Suddenly a herd of horses come galloping over the hill straight towards us, perhaps 70, they roll in the dirt and drink from the river, they are right next to us, it is a sight to remember!!! A van pulls up, it is full of people in traditional dress, they come and say hello....

Monday 9th August........153833........Today we drive the river valley, horses and cattle everywhere, the roads are really bad again. Beverley spots another tea cup, just sitting there on its own, nobody could accuse her of not paying attention to detail !!!...

We see huge eagles about 3ft in height, the locals catch and train these huge birds to hunt for them. We go over a bridge crossing a very wide, deep river, after we have crossed Beverley tells me the sign said 1 ton........ we're more like 3 ton!!!...

2.30pm. The sat nav says 3.30pm, so we have crossed another time line...now 7 hours ahead. Driving up higher there are lots of dead trees, it is cold and rainy, we stop for a while, me and Beverley walk up to the top of the hill, the plants look the same as you would see in an alpine rockery. Back down and we meet a shepherd, his saddle is made of wood, he calls to his cattle, fascinating..

There is a storm coming so we drive on a bit longer.....then we see two people on a motorbike with a roof, it's an amazing vehicle, we stop for a chat, they are Karen and Kevin from Surrey......www.guzzioverland.co.uk. Small world, wc have tea and exchange stories, wonderful.

Tuesday 10th August.........153931......we are doing about 15mph, that's as fast as the track will allow, there are roads being built here, they are unusable but easy to follow, it spoils it a bit-----too easy!!!

We see Karen and Kevin again and stop for cup of tea, it's great to be able to just have a chat.

There are lots of children by the sides of the roads trying to sell milk and blueberries, we buy a bottle of the milk, just because we can, we have no use for it, except to see the smile on the childs face.

We see an unfinished road and drive onto it, tarmac, it's like driving on silk. There are steep banks to stop you being able to get to the road, but James is quite capable. Not far along we come to a road roller and the driver tries to block our path. We drive over the pile of dirt at the end of the section, but not fast enough----we are stuck!!! Darren calls to the driver of the road roller to come and give us a shove, and he does, quite a hard shove, we are free, the price being a bent door with broken glass, oh well!!

Wednesday 11th August......154040.......average speed 15mph again. We arrive at a town and start to see signs of tourism. Dreamland Resort, it is made up of the Mongolian tents –Gers. The area is called Orkhon National Park----there is also a shop called United Food Corporation.

Further along, Darren fills up the diesel tank from the jerry can and then we drive off without putting the cap back on. All of a sudden Darren realises this, we stop to look for the cap ,we spend forever searching for it, walking up and down the road, but it has disappeared. Another remedy is found to cover the open pipe.

We start to make camp, a family in a car pull up, all climb out of their wagon, perhaps eight of them. They all come to inspect us, and our tents, climbing up the ladders to peer into the tents, what a sight we must be. We give them the milk we bought earlier, and they are delighted... lovely people.......

Thursday 12th August.....154138.....very windy, the tent folded on us but no harm done! We travel over miles and miles of flat plains, with herds of horses, cattle, goats, and sheep....we see a dead horse with a dog eating it, with the eagles waiting their turn.....

Driving towards the capital we start to see agriculture and fences and tarmac. Arriving in Ulaanbaatar town we find Oasis, the travellers guest house that we were told about by a couple of German travellers. When we checked in we were told that they knew we were coming because Ian, who we met in Astana, had just left. We rent a ger, it has a fire in it, the food is good and the company is brilliant, all travellers' tales.........

Friday 13th August......154306......Slept well. There is a profusion of spiders living on the walls of the ger. They crawl all over our beds, and as we lie down, our faces, really creepy. I believe they are harmless, or we would have been warned, you need to just turn off and ignore them, such fun!

When we drove out of Oasis and saw A&A parked outside an hotel, we stop to say hello and direct them to Oasis, they knew about the place but were unable to find it. We drive around exploring..........

Saturday 14th August.......quiet day just meeting folk....there are two French men who want to spend time with us, because we know how to play ballot, a card game we used to play with our neighbours in Villajou----good fun......

Sunday 15th August. We visit the Natural History museum to see the dinosaur bones that have been found in the Gobi desert, interesting. Back at base we meet more people, including Mel, a young French lady on a motorbike, Betty and Gerald from the Netherlands,, 4 lads from England who have driven here in an ambulance. The lads have raised

£5000 for charity and then they will donate the ambulance and fly back. Darren walks us to black market and buys a spare tyre for £80.....

Monday 16th August.....We drive across town to immigration, with A& A to extend our visas so that the dates fit with our China entry----no problems for us. Agnes has upset the immigration officer by tapping on the desk, in a gesture for him to hurry up. Now they have the wrong date, they have to leave Mongolia on the 15th and enter China on the 16th. This could be a big problem for us all as we have to enter China together.

Tuesday 17th August......we go to black market again to buy some clothes----while we are there someone steals our new spare tyre!!!!

Wednesday 18th August.....It rained all night, again, weather is rotten so we stay another day. We drive to Laos embassy to buy visas, the policeman on duty, outside the gate, is fast asleep, we had to wake him up. We get the paperwork but need another couple of passport photos, so back to camp and we go for a walk to find somewhere to buy photos. Whilst walking we are able to see just how dirty and grimy Ulaanbaatar really is. It's been raining all day, the drains are inadequate, the roads are all flooded, and there is rubbish and rats everywhere.

Thursday 19th August.....154396........We have been invited to a French Bistro by Pierre and Mark, so we have stayed yet another extra day. The weather is good and we have been able to air the tents, all ok and dry.

Darren goes out for a steak, but Beverley is not well at all, so we stay behind. It's horrible seeing your child ill, but in a place like this it's frightening, it makes me question our journey.

We have been warned to stay away from the slums as there is another outbreak of the black plague! That news doesn't fill me with confidence!

On return Darren tells me it was the best steak he has ever had!!

Friday 20th August....154413.....On the road for 10.45am. I'm glad to say that Beverley has a better colour today, thank goodness.

Back through the mad city, non- stop car horns, people with no fear at all about being hit by a car, they just walk straight out. Police whistles, people driving with children on their laps while chatting on mobile phones -- pollution -- so many cars, most of the time it is jammed. We are trying to head N.W. to a large freshwater lake....12.10pm we have managed 7 miles so far, nothing is moving. Further on in the town, where most of the people live, it is slums with no running water or sewage, this must be where we were warned against, it seems we have been staying in the nice part of town!!! 1pm we are out of the city and have done a total of 21 miles....(I think in this case the use of the word slum is tolerable)...

90 miles further on by the side of road (dirt track) we make camp for the night, high up a mountain, surrounded by herds of horses..........feels good to be out of the city in the fresh air.

Saturday 21st August....154524.......4.15pm still heading N.W. on a very rough track.

Sunday 22nd August.......154666......Good camp last night, back on the road for 11.45am. Open plains and many, many animals. Then tree lined tracks, if you saw pictures of here, you could easily think it was Greece or Turkey!!!! Then open plains and thick forests......

Monday 23rd August.....154778......Hot!!! Trying to make a breakfast in the back seat of this Landy is like a new sport----extreme sandwich making!!! 2.20pm we arrive at the town of Meren and get supplies.......5pm we see a sign to tell us we are entering a national park, here they have wild cat, elk, rare fish and gold but it states any gold found cannot be taken home........

Tuesday 24th August....154886......Still going with an average speed 10mph. We come to a beautiful river, we drive through and park up for a cup of tea, and to do the washing. The water is crystal clear, we are quite high up a mountain and we are completely lost, we should of been by the lake by now but must have taken a wrong turning. It really does not matter to us we can just enjoy where we are. We could ask the locals, but that would include having to drink the salty, milky tea. We camp in a beautiful valley ...

Wednesday 25th August.....154956......We wake up to see a herd of the very hairy cows ambling past us, Beverley gets some photos. They are so lovely to watch, the cute babies, and when the adults run they look like they are running of the tips of their toes......

We decide to follow our tracks back to Meren, we stop at a market for some fresh veg. and we meet a couple of backpackers from Israel. Meanwhile, back at the Landy, Beverley has met three Frenchmen and is busily chatting away in French to them

Darren has a look at the Landy, we decide it is best to head back to Ulaanbaatar as poor old James is suffering -- the exterior cage-(-the scaffold bars) are taking a battering, one is nearly split all the way through.

We set off and see a group of seven motorbikes, we stop and have a chat with the support team, a lady from Sydney and a man from Germany. They are a little taken aback when we tell them we are on our own, no support team, no phone coverage, nothing, just each other.

A bit further on we see a Mongolian man picking up bits from the road, his motorbike and a lady stand at the side.....we stop and offer help, he refuses and insists he is ok. At first he looks like he has a terrible skin infection and comes over to shake hands, then we can see his face is full of gravel from the road, he thanks us and says it is nothing!!!!

Thursday 26th August.......155101.....Last night Beverley became ill again, and has been sick so we stay put and let her rest...by 3pm she feels better, although she is far from right.

We move off...at 6pm we find some tarmac...poor James, the shock absorber has pulled right through the axle mounting, and another UJ needs changing!!!!!

Friday 27th August......155212........We all get up early so that we can get to Ulaanbaatar today, off by 8.30am.....Beverley is still ill, poor girl. The car is rolling like a boat with loud clangs and bangs every so often, just what you don't need if you feel sick. She wants to get back to the Oasis guest house and the Mongolian tent. We head back a different way, east through Erdenet city, hoping it might be tarmac all the way. It is supposed to be a lovely city between mountains and two rivers, but to me it has ugly hot water pipes everywhere and a huge electric power station, it is a mining city, a Russian/Mongolian development and it shows, still as long as there is tarmac for James.

Suddenly a lorry pulls out in front of us, Darren swerves and we just make it past, Darren is brilliant. I think if I had been driving we would have been off the road, good job I'm not!!!!

1.45pm arriving at outskirts of Ulaanbaatar. I am sorting out our money, piles of notes, there are no coins here. I have one note which is worth about half a penny. We pay to enter each city, some towns. and bridges but it is not much; perhaps 25p to a £1.

2.45pm We have crossed the city and arrived back at the travellers guest house again, luckily they have an empty ger, which we take. Now Beverley can go to bed, and hopefully she will be fit in the morning.........

Saturday 28th August.......At Oasis....Beverley is a lot better and keeps talking about food and asking if you can get vegetable pasties in Oz., We spend an hour or so, working on the Landy ,and then Beverley is sick again, so we stay in the Ger.......

Sunday 29th August....At Oasis.....Beverley better!!! What a relief!!!!!!!!

Darren starts on the car repairs, we go down the black market to get bits. I find suitcases for storage, they are cheaper than the plastic boxes and they might even keep out a bit of the Gobi desert. Some of our original plastic boxes are falling to bits, but I think they have been through a lot and done very well.

Back at Oasis we meet an English couple, Helen and Paul, they are on a two year round the world tour. Plenty of chatting and stories to share, we work on the car again, for a while, and then all go for a pizza together........

Monday 30th August...At Oasis.... Two Dutch couples are leaving today on their quad bikes. When they reach Moscow they are going to break the world record for the distance travelled on a quad.

Lunchtime we go on the bus to town, for lunch with Graham, an English motorcyclist. We meet him in a Irish pub, where he says the food is good--he is right!! We hitch a lift back to Oasis, and spend more time on the car. Beverley is fit, but tired after our trip into town. She stays in the tent and plays runescape on the computer and checks her facebook account--happy!

Tuesday 31st August.....At Oasis....Darren has done an unbelievable job on the Landy, he has replaced the worn scaffold bars with wood, and the first roof tent is back on....

Helen and Paul have come up from the Gobi desert, from the places we want to visit, so we check out routes on our maps. They have been sponsored by a lot of different groups which seems to take them hours to do reports and videos. Having to think all the time of what the sponsors want. I'm glad we didn't go down that line, we seem to be busy all the time just sorting ourselves out.

I had a long chat with Sybil, she runs Oasis, with her husband Rene. Originally, they came here 15 years ago working for charities. The local people rely on them for hot showers and washing machines, and many other things, they do a wonderful job.

Wednesday 1st September 2010. Starting our 6th month on the road....At Oasis.

We went to the black market to buy bits for the car. Watching people make gaskets and buckets out of the old tyres--brilliant ideas--they don't waste anything.

Darren gets the second tent up but hits the windscreen and cracks it. It will have to hold because there is no replacement for it, should be ok!! The sand-boards are now fixed on the bonnet.........

Thursday 2nd September...At Oasis......We go to the Laos embassy to drop of forms and passport, will pick up visas tomorrow. Back to black the market and Beverley buys two new pairs of trousers one bright yellow pair for £1.25 and a bright green pair for £2, she likes to wear the brightest colours she can find, all mixed up, it's great, she really stands out, it's good fun. Worked on car and spent time chatting == love it........

Friday 3rd September...At Oasis......155476......Darren goes to Laos embassy and picks up visas, all ok...We shower and start to pack, again. We have lunch and say our goodbyes and leave at 1.40pm....

Back on the road again, heading south for the Gobi desert. Out of Ulaanbaatar and the tarmac ends...4.30pm and the exhaust vibrates loose again---Darren fixes all ok. The tents, now screwed onto wood which is screwed through the roof; with wood supports off the gutter, good and solid, skilful job!!

We go up the mountains, at the top of each is a pile of stones with blue cloths on. I believe we are supposed to drive round each one, three times, for good luck. Then there is miles and miles of track, in the distance, till the next peak, and so on. The roads are corrugated and every so often we actually take off........

6pm we stop next to a mountain peak with hills all around, for a bit of protection. This is desert, but where the Gobi officially starts--if it does-- who knows. It is 32 degrees in the car, the sun is shining, and it starts to rain, not really what you would expect. We get a beautiful double rainbow. The land appears pinky, orange with odd bushes and a thin covering of tiny plants. Two dogs come to visit, Darren chases them away, they look a bit yucky and we know that they can carry all kinds of diseases out here. As it starts to get dark we can see the dogs slowly creeping closer, we've thrown all our scraps out for them, a fair distance from the landy...........

Saturday 4th September......155565.....Good night, it's nice to be back in the tents. The wind is very strong.   Darren struggles to put the tents down, it's a good job he is so strong.

 On the road for 9am.   Sunny.   We think we took a wrong turn yesterday, can't be sure.   11am the track we are on is taking us S.W. We follow faint tracks which take us to a ger camp, there are no other tracks that we can see, so we make fresh ones and head off S. S.E....

The bushes, of which there were many, have now disappeared, and the land is coloured by tiny plants that cover huge areas, it appears red and orange, green and purple, beautiful!!

Out comes the hand held compass, just to verify our route.

We see remnants of bones, I was told that last winter was minus 50 degrees and the different animals huddled together, and died together, and this explains the piles of different bones.

We drive to the brow of a hill and see nothing, no tracks or signs of life. Another brow and another, until eventually we find a track. Hundreds of birds take off as we drive through, they look like a cross between a duck and a pigeon, light brown, fawny, sandy coloured like the desert. I make a note to google them next time we have internet!!! We drive through a dried up watering hole and past a huge crater which looks like it could of been a lake, long ago, who knows? We see abandoned buildings, a herd of camels, we drive over a dried up river bed, more camels..

12pm....We think about one to one and a half hours to the town we are heading for. One ger in the distance, then we see a shepherd with a herd of horses, we stop on the track for a five minute break, the first car we have seen today is coming towards us..

Me and Beverley take a walk to see what we can find, we see one green spider cricket, no others, we kick over stone after stone but only find one small spider, it is silent, no birds or crickets singing.......

Off again, at the top of one hill we see a bucket on top of a long pole and on another a very large milk churn with rocks in it, and a few skulls around it? Then in the distance we see a communications mast, we must be getting close now.

2.20pm We arrive at the town, we buy supplies and off we go.....4.30pm the desert is so flat...there are blue rocks everywhere.....6pm we stop in the sand dunes, this is real sand, Beverley spots a little lizard and grabs the camera, it's skin looks like grains of sand. There are lots of bones around, a strange looking bone sticks out of the sand, I have to dig it up to find out what it is, a goats head complete with horns. Well this is the desert where all the dinosaur bones have been found, you have to try!!! 8.10pm getting dark, just finished eating, time for a film on our faithful laptop, it's still a hot 30 degrees......

Sunday 5th September........155751........Terrific wind last night, glad we were in the sand dunes they gave us a little protection.

10am on road...11.20am found a track which leads us to a small town. Corrugated roads, it's so flat it's like looking at the sea. 12.30pm we find a well, so I do the washing, fill up water tanks. Then we have a visitor, one lonely camel comes walking slowly towards us, he or she is as curious as us. We all stand still and study each other, we can see his thick hairy thighs, he has fur right down to his feet. He slowly makes his way over to the water and drinks, Beverley and Darren stroke him, a fantastic experience.....

Back on the road and another storm, raining, lightning. I try to concentrate on reading a book so I don't see all the lightning, it helps a bit, but I can still hear the tremendously loud thunder.

We see gazelles running, it's a wonderful sight. Then Beverley spots a dead hedgehog in the road, didn't expect to see hedgehogs. We stop for a rest.......thunder, lightning, sand blowing across the corrugated road. Off again, there are piles of bones by the side of the road, hope we don't join them!

We come to the town we were looking for, we pass through and drive deep into the mountains. We come across a camp with tents and cars, but there is no way past, it's the end of the road, so it's back towards town. We find another track going west, we will try this one.

It is still raining, as it has every day since we arrived in the Gobi!!!!

Monday 6th September......155877.....Last night we could find no shelter, there was nothing to see in all directions, a very windy night!!

8am. Freezing cold and windy, by 10am we are back on the road. We pass a pile of rocks with a horses head on top. It is surrounded by a huge stack of bones, and bits, of, perhaps, dozens of animals?

The land is changing colour, it appears yellow. We are heading for the mountains through a dried up river basin, lines of green grassy plants follow the tracks. Along the side of the tracks there are huge holes in the ground, the land has collapsed, it looks like cliffs. We see one lonely ger and a few horses. Another thunderstorm and lightning. The sand is changing to mud....Darren is loving it, and as he says, I am having kittens in the back!!!! We cross streams, which if the rain continues I think they will revert to rivers......

We want to continue to travel to what we have been told are the enormous sand dunes, but it's not the same in the cold pouring rain. By 11.30am we have decided to turn back and go east towards the China crossing, in the hope the weather will improve.

We cross a fast running, pure orange coloured stream, which is a lot bigger than when we crossed it 20 minutes ago!!!! 1pm we are back on the plain. We came back on a different route that I thought was even more scary than the way into the mountains.

Darren says that this is what Mongolia is all about, getting off road and not knowing where you are----fun! I agree but could do without the storms!! (My reaction to all this fun is little blisters all over my hands).

Beverley doesn't bat an eyelid. The sun shines, looking back at mountains, we can't see them, they are covered by black cloud.

Driving east through sand dunes, we notice there are pieces of coal everywhere. We come to a mining village, it's cold and rainy again....

Tuesday 7th September.....156010.......rained nearly all night and it was cold. The rain stopped just long enough to put the tents down. Drove all day, stopped at one small town for supplies.....

5pm pulled up in the sand dunes, as far as we can see, in all directions, there is nothing, no signs of life at all, it's a strange lonely feeling. Nobody in the world knows we are here and we have no connection with anyone, kind of exciting too!.

We get out the television and the wii machine. We built a shelter with the tarpaulins----perfect. Determined to have fun, even if it keeps raining. After just 6 minutes the television slipped and fell on the wii and the screen broke...the telly had lasted 9 months in the car and travelled approx 20,000 miles!!!!

Huge windstorm again...

Wednesday 8th September....156124....Rained all night, 10.30am sitting in car, Beverley on computer, Darren playing nintendo and me doing crosswords. If the rain stops we will move on, if not we will stay for a day or so. Grey miserable sky, not a break in it anywhere. Question ---what is the definition of a desert? 12pm still the same..and 5pm...and 7pm...and 10.30pm..bed.....

Thursday 9th September.....8.30 am sunny, rushing to do tents, black clouds arriving. James is holding up well, except for one of the spotlights, all the insides have fallen out!!

There is water everywhere, we slide, and then sink, we dig our way out with the sand-boards. We see a motorbike, stuck, and we go to help them, we get them out, then we sink again!! They help us dig out and after about an hour we are out. We spend about half an hour walking in front of the landy, trying to pick out the driest route. The soaking wet sand sucks at our feet, we just about make it out onto a drier bit when two lorries arrive and one gets stuck!!! Half an hour and we are all moving . It's like driving up a river. The road, if you can call it that goes on and on, after a while we see pylons!!! Next we see camels and we realise that we must of seen thousands of them on our travels, some with ropes or head collars or harnesses, but we have never seen one being ridden or actually doing anything.....

This is not how any of us pictured our visit to the Gobi desert. Sinking, digging ourselves, and others out. Torrential rain, grey skies, black fearsome clouds. It would be very easy to get stuck for good, nobody would know---best not to think that way....

We see strange shapes in the distance, as we get closer we recognise them--- trees! 3.30pm. Arrive at small town, they have no fruit, no beer, no supplies at all, so we carry on........

Friday 10th September.....We are in the area of Dorngobi in a town called Sjansand, and yesterday we found the hotel Dorngobi, it is clean and £20 a night for a room with two double beds..tv..and hot shower, can you imagine the look on mine and Beverleys face? They also do laundry, I think I might treat myself and let someone else do it. The laundry lady, who wore a huge hair-do and an evening dress, inspected our laundry wearing her rubber gloves and tutting loudly at each piece of washing. She then announced that she wanted £25 for the load...£8 for a couple of days undies, no thank-you. I shall wash them myself in the bathroom. I find it hard to believe that, yesterday we were in the middle of a desert, and today we are in a snooty hotel, weird!

We go down to dinner to find it very busy with many people. We haven't seen so many people for a long time! Lots of speeches and Mongolian singing---free entertainment for us. We have no idea what its all about. The meal is---how shall I say this--- barely edible. Mongolian fare, it seems they cook without using any salt or herbs, it is all so plain and full of fat. We walked into town and ate at the 'best' restaurant, they speak no English but that's no problem, unfortunately the food is just the same!!!

Saturday 11th September......At the hotel, on the balcony, we can see all the schoolchildren in uniforms marching, for hours. They are dressed in white shirts, the different ages having different styles, to us the older girls look like French maids---

We watched a bit of Lord of the rings..in Mongolian.......We meet two couples, American and English, they have been teaching English in Korea for a year and have flown in for a tour round before going home....Kian comes into our room for a game on the wii, it's good to have company..

Sunday 12th September. From the balcony we watched old cars passing, dozens of them, all classics. It's the Peking to Paris rally. We also watched the Italian grand prix, on a Russian tv channel.

Monday 13th September....156265 - Up early, and we are off again. There are masses of flies that keep landing on us, so annoying! We drive until we are 25 miles from the border and camp. We are not going to get any closer to the border town after our last experience.

Tuesday 14th September....156370.......Good, warm quiet night. We have driven just over 17,000 miles since April 1st.

We drive to the border and take a look around the town, returning back to desert for another day. We are keeping a look out for A&A, they should arrive soon.

Wednesday 15h September.....156404.....Just waiting around to cross the border, it's raining again. A& A have to leave Mongolia today so we were expecting them last night or early this morning, should see them before long. ....

2pm A &A arrive, the car covered in thick mud. We think, perhaps, they may have got stuck in the desert, like us. They explain that, they have remained on the main road, on the tarmac, through-out their visit.

3pm straight through the Mongolian passport control....

4pm China.. We are told that there is no guide until tomorrow - big problem!!!! Agnes had e-mailed the guide and told them we will arrive on the 15th, but has had no internet connection for a few days and didn't think to contact them again until now. The guide replies and says she arrived this morning, as arranged, but no-one was at the border, and she had had no contact from Agnes, so she left. She will come again tomorrow morning.

 The guards tell us we cannot stay here, and we cannot go back, and we cannot drive into China without a guide.

After a couple of hours they come up with an alternative, we can enter on foot....we lock the cars and take what we need , we enter passport control and start the process. It is now 6 o'clock -- closing time for customs - the electric is cut off before we have been processed, what next?

The guards are so friendly and all smiles, they tell us not to worry. The next thing, we are getting into their mini-bus, they take us to an ATM, then we are taken for a meal. They take us upstairs in the café, we have our own table in a booth, they help us to order, after a wonderfully tasty meal, they walk us to a hotel, give us back our passports ,(according to which we have not entered China yet) and say 'see you in the morning,' fantastic, we are so impressed, these people are lovely and seem so happy. We can tell we are being watched closely in the hotel, but we can't blame them, the trouble we could cause if we disappeared!

This is the first hotel, of many, as we are only allowed to stay in hotels with our guide, no camping allowed.

Thursday 16th September......156430.......Out for tea and breakfast at a cafe. We don't have any idea what we are ordering, there are no pictures to point at. It arrives as fried fish and noodles, afterwards we go and buy bread and fruit for Beverley

Our guide arrives, she is a 22 year old student, called Angel. She tells us that this is her first time as a guide. Off we all go, back to customs, we are asked to wait in the guards rest room, very nice. Our passports are sorted, then we go straight through passport control.....

We have heard many horror stories about this crossing, how it can take all day, with the cars being completely stripped.

Darren and Alan go to the cars, they are sent to the front of the queue and off we go, to the government hotel, while we wait for our Chinese number plates, insurance etc., Lovely hotel - great rooms and gorgeous beds, all for £20 a night for a double room---plus breakfast. We all agree they can take as long as they like with the paperwork, to have soft carpet to walk on is something we had forgotten about--sheer luxury!!!!!

Friday 17th September.......156434.......Had breakfast and took a walk, came back in a rickshaw, it was electric!!! Angel has left to sort out the paperwork. Checked out of the hotel and cooked lunch at the Landy.

 We are waiting for Angel in the hotel car park, thus avoiding paying for another day at the hotel not knowing how long she will be. She arrives at 4pm with everything sorted...off to Beijing!!!

Erlion is a huge border town with exquisite flat tarmac going out into the desert; we see sheep, camels, wild horses It's pouring with rain, but we don't care, this is so exciting..

 Along the side of the road are hundreds of life size dinosaurs, depicting what has been found here, it's a wonderful display........We drive on for hours in the dark. Our lights are not working properly, just the main beam. At 9.30pm we stop at a cheap hotel, basic but ok, £16 for the night for all 8 off us. We walk in the rain and find a restaurant, just about to close, but they will stay open for us, we all have a lovely meal. Except for Beverley, vegetarian seems to have a different meaning here, you can be a chicken vege or a fish vege, it was like that in France. Luckily Beverley loves rice, and the Jasmine tea.

Saturday 18th September...156589......Overcast but dry, on the road for 9am...We are still in the Gobi but so different from Mongolia, there is agriculture, trees, tarmac roads and even road signs!

12pm lunch at a very pretty hotel, as Beverley said, the interior was just like disneyland, a lovely meal for 8 £30. Angel explains there are no tips, as the waitresses are very well paid, perhaps £120 a month......

2.30pm Back on road. The hills are terraced, there is food growing everywhere, we see many wind turbines, it feels like we have jumped forward a century!!!

5.30pm We see the Great Wall stretching out across the tops of the mountains---awesome. As we enter Beijing we play Katie Melua..."There are nine million bicycles in Beijing", we have been told that Beijing, including suburbs, is the same size as Belgium. Angel takes us to the middle of town, to a hotel---£70 a night for all 3 rooms.

We walked along the river, bars and restaurants by the dozen, had a pleasant meal......

Darren writes "China so far has turned out to be the real highlight for me, Beijing is exactly what I expected, just so many people, after coming through Mongolia it's such a culture shock, I'm so pleased to be doing the journey this way as to go from here to Mongolia would be such a let down. The car is behaving itself no problems at all"

Sunday 19th September....Taxi to Tiananmen Square and then the Imperial Palace, the Forbidden city. These two are both places you have to visit, because they are so famous, it's exciting for that reason, but all I can say is, we've been there!!

Next to a shopping mall and we bought new tv so we can play wii, got a very good price. The dvd's are £3 each brand new!! Back to the hotel by tube train, which was good fun and then taxi to a restaurant. The people, Angel works for, have offered to buy us a meal. They are waiting for payment from us, I'm sure this has nothing to do with it!

Monday 20th September.....156835......Went to the famous Silk market, it's enormous and you have to barter for everything. The banter is so friendly, such good fun--Darren is brilliant at it, we buy new boots for Beverley, and lots of T. shirts and more dvd's, they didn't make much profit out of us, Darren knocked those prices down!!!!

Angel does not seem to be herself, we question her, and it appears she has had a phone call to say she is being replaced as they do not think she is experienced enough for the journey. We think different and tell them so, and if they want the rest of their money to leave things as they are......they say ok!!!!

Tuesday 21st September....Get up early to see Tai Chi in the park, but it's raining so nobody there. We arrive at the Great Wall at 7.30am, the ticket office is open ,otherwise the place is deserted, nobody else there, got it to ourselves!!

Me, Beverley and Angel get to where they say you are a hero for climbing so far and decide that's enough for us. Agnes and Darren carry on---the crowds are now starting to climb up. By 9.30am we are back at the car, although a bit wet, we are very pleased with our achievement -- the crowds fill the steps now....It's hard to take in what we have just done!!!!

Off to Datong to see the caves, on the way we stop for lunch--donkey sandwiches!! This is a coal mining area and we see bits of black in our tea cups....

5pm stop at Datong Phoenix Hotel--very nice--£20 a room, we draw crowds again, interested by the look of us.

Wednesday 22nd September...Darren and Alan do repairs to the two Landies, parked in the street, in front of the hotel. Beverley counted 68 people watching them. Darren got an inner tube fixed at the corner of street, by a bicycle repair man, for 50 pence......

Today is the mid autumn harvest moon festival and we are given moon cakes, so generous. In the afternoon we visited the Yungang Grottoes, (at the base of the Wuzhou Shan mountains) the grotto took 68 years to create, there are over 51.000 Buddas. Some are hundreds of feet high, others just a few inches, there are 252 grottos, it's fascinating--- They say that the river got in the way, so they moved it, and redirected it. All this in the 5th and 6th centuries, the Chinese are definitely not shy of hard work.

This was a good place for David and June to have a run about and enjoy a bit of freedom, which is always good to see. After building up a good appetite, we go downtown for an evening meal, which consisted of fried chicken bones in batter, very tasty but I would of preferred the meat. Beverley had more boiled rice and vegies.

Went to Walmart to buy bread, sounds like were in America!

Thursday 23rd September......157045.......Crowds of people watch as we prepare to leave, Agnes has trouble getting into her car with so many people in her way. We go onto the toll road, where there are cars on the wrong side of the carriageway. It seems to be normal here to see vehicles heading towards you!!!

Up into mountains, lovely new roads, lots of donkey carts, flowers and shrubs at the side of the roads, everywhere is so clean. We go through an old town and see the oldest wooden tower in China- apparently in the world, although I can't help thinking we've seen the oldest tower in the world in another country as well!!!! The sun is setting as we arrive in Taiyuan. We found a lovely hotel, after a great meal, we go upstairs with our new dvd player and watch Star Wars on the hotels large flat screen tv.......

Friday 24th September....157247...... We've got grey skies but it's warm. Buy supplies from a supermarket, including Dorian fruit, known as stink fruit, and it does. We thought we must try it, very sweet, well at least we tried it. Angel takes it to A &A's car and eats it in the back, can't help smiling!!!

We drive to an ancient walled city—the oldest in China-at Pingyau. It's a living museum, cobbled roads, tiled roofs, many with added details, such as, the end of each roof tile has a face, or a pattern on it. We can see into backyards with all the furniture of everyday life. ---

A & A lost little David, they both thought he was with each other, after a good scare he turns up smiling, cheeky boy!

Then it's onto the motorway, it travels through mountains, under and over and around them. It's an unbelievable achievement. The scenery is out of this world, steppes on mountains, again food everywhere!!!

We arrive at a hotel with the staff all dressed in traditional clothes, they open doors for us and bow!!! What an outstanding place....

Saturday 25th September....157410.....9.30am and we are on the road to see the waterfall on the Yellow river. Up the mountain roads into the clouds, there are cars with no lights on, it's difficult to see them coming.

We see people hand digging coal at a power station, the pollution is thick in the air, these people cannot have a long life expectancy. I wander what the English health and safety board would make of this place?

The sun breaks through and we arrive at the waterfall, we park and walk to buy tickets. It is well worth it, what a sight, the waterfall is extremely powerful, we walk across wet rocks and sand to look down on it---awesome. It is hard to explain, but our feet are level with the rapids, just in front of us, it would be very easy to fall in, there would be nothing left of you, if you hit those rocks with such a force of water, incredible. The water is brown, coloured by all the silt, not exactly yellow, it's a breath-taking sight.

Back at the Landy, I cook mashed potato; it's like giving a master-class to a spellbound audience!!!.... Well, thinking about it, this is China, they eat rice not mash, I would love to offer a taste, but so many people are watching, there just isn't enough to share.

3.30pm off to Xian to see the Terracotta army--it is over 300k so will, perhaps, do half today. It is all a bit of a rush, we are only allowed 30 days to cross China, which doesn't leave much time for visits, and we are supposed to stay on the government approved routes.

6.30pm We come off the motorway for a hotel for the night .Whoops we are the first non-Chinese to visit this town, the police arrive and Darren goes with them, they want to copy all our visas for Russia etc. They want to know exactly where we have been...Darren says "No".. they do not have the right to ask these questions or to copy visas. Darren takes the copies off them, our Chinese visa gives us permission to be here, Darren explains this and they have to agree and let him leave. We think they are just very curious as they have not seen any westerners before, we are not supposed to leave the planned route, and are expected to just drive through the night, but to hell with it, we have hungry, tired children, who need to get out of their chairs......great hotel with everything £10 a room.

Sunday 26th September......157615...... My Dads birthday, I never dreamt, I would miss his birthday because I was in China, wish I could see him! Happy birthday Dad.

10am and it's sunny and warm, fabulous views over mountains, some of the houses are built into the mountainside and caves....

12.45pm arrive at Xian, it's a huge city, there are hundreds of trees down the middle of the roads and they are all being fed by drips. You can taste the pollution in the air---buses, cars, markets, people--we find a Super 8 hotel, it's good and so is the pizza we find!!!

Monday 27th September.....157718.....10.20am off to Lintong for the Terracotta Army. masses of traffic. It seems that the traffic lights are optional, the only rule is biggest vehicle first, a taxi drives into us, no damage to us but he is most put out and follows us trying to pull in front for an argument, He tries to stop A & A by driving in front of them, but they are having none of it, he drove into us --so we just ignore him and after a while he drives off !!

We spend a brilliant day looking at all the statues and diggings, the size of the plot is astounding, there are three vast halls.

It's a collection of statues, an army for the first Emperor of China- to protect him in his afterlife, and for him to rule, estimated at 8000 soldiers, 130 chariots with 520 horses and 150 cavalry horses, most of which are still buried. There was also entertainment planned with acrobats and musicians, and others, he was obviously expecting to be very busy! They date back to the 3rd century BC. They were discovered by a farmer digging in his field in 1974, they had all been broken and buried by the following, probably jealous, Emperor.

Tuesday 28th September....157778.....10am, warm with grey polluted skies, off to Chengdu and the pandas., can't wait! Through the mountains, the forests looking thicker than ever--at 2.25pm we see a sign saying Panda Habitat Zone!!! Passing through forests, which really is now jungle, the sort we have not seen before except with David Attenborough. Beverley spots banana trees, we are still on toll roads that are smooth and every couple of miles there is a person in an orange jacket sweeping the road!! Off the toll road and it's dark dangerous roads into town - Gungywan, where there is China's biggest nuclear reactor. The hotel insists on us filling in form after form, it's horrible here---the rooms have insects, Angel is terrified and changes room three times, we are used to camping so a bit tougher---the water smells like eggs - enough said!!

Wednesday 29th September......158017.....Lovely sunny day, we see rice fields, massive pampas grass, banana trees---260k to Chengdu---

12.30pm We stop--a car has crashed into a van, the people inside are hurt but they refuse any help from us, other vehicles have stopped so we continue on.......

Angel has booked us into a hotel called Holiday Sunshine, we hope it will be better than last night.

 No! It's crap and to add to it they won't take foreigners or aliens as they call us, maybe they are not allowed to by law – who knows!.....

We go just next door, to the Yale Hotel--it is lovely with no problems.......we go for a meal---Hot pot which is a local favourite but it is so hot even Darren can't enjoy it!!!

Thursday 30th September.....Watch videos in hotel--go for lunch - chips and pizza for which they give us knives and forks and Beverley notices that on the back of them it says 'made in Japan'. There are flowers everywhere here and it smells lovely even above all the traffic....

Friday 1st October.......8.20am we follow a taxi with Angel in it, it's the quickest way to get out of this big city, and find the panda sanctuary!!

Today is the first day of the national 10 day holiday so we expect queues. We soon arrive, it wasn't far at all, it's raining, but that's good the pandas like it. We enter the panda sanctuary hoping to be able to see one or two. There's no chance in the wild, unless you want to sit for days waiting, like the wildlife photographers, the pandas are out there, but so are millions of other life forms that I don't want to come into contact with.

There they are, outside, mostly eating, some sleeping up trees, some playing, it's brilliant to see them all, including four babies, they are so cute and the aaaahhhh factor is huge!!!! Pandas in China, is this real? Wow! We all just stare and take photos for ages, oh! this is breath-taking, awe-inspiring, I feel really proud of us all for being here.....what a terrific day to remember!

We have trouble finding hotel rooms, because of the holiday, and A & A's financial limitations. Angel investigates the area, talking to many people, where would we be without her? Eventually she finds three rooms, up a flight of dirty concrete steps at the back of a market. This is not an hotel but a place where adults may choose to spend an hour or two, (a knocking shop). We end up with a tatty room and a smelly pit toilet. Checking the room out we find one double bed, with an offer of another mattress on the floor, the en=suite bathroom makes me heave as soon as the door is partly opened. It's just one night, which really is only a few hours, this is how Beverley and me talk to each other. Again Darrens' total lack of a sense of smell, is envied by all. A&A's room has a round bed with pink sheets, (so obvious what this place is) at least their children arc too young to understand ----- just one night!!

Saturday 2nd October.....158290......Heading for Litang, the farthest west and the nearest to Tibet we are allowed to go. Up mountain roads, the insect noise is now so loud it drones out the sound of the Landrover engines, and that's saying something., We see kiwi fruit and wood carvings for sale by the ton.....

Sunday 3rd October.....158370.......Up the mountain road, which is half closed because part of it has collapsed. It's a gamble when two cars pass as to whether the road will hold up!

Cars passing us covered in snow!! 11200ft.. and although it's getting colder I am starting to sweat due to the altitude, and we are getting headaches.... I make sandwiches and the sauce explodes out of the bottle, I suppose I should of expected that!!!

We are driving at approx. 12km per hour, repeatedly stopping for traffic jams, and lots of really mindless drivers, some of which seem to have a death wish!!!

The houses have changed, they are square with beautifully intricately painted, colourful doors and windows, mainly two floors high with roof terraces, makes me think of Peru.----faces also have changed--longer faces with much darker skin, quite different.........

The only hotel we can find has one room with eight beds in it---(we cannot camp, there is nowhere to go). There is a communal pit toilet on the landing, which after being forced to use, I am sick into the bin, there was no- where else!!!! Yuk!!! Beverley and June are feeling ill---David is sick.....we all have bad headaches--------- The lack of oxygen is affecting us all. I am dizzy, and have basically lost control of both ends. Beverley is the most fantastic nurse. In the early morning, while there is no-one around, me and Beverley go outside so we don't have to go to that toilet again....... Evcryone gets up feeling rough, we need to get down lower. We are now at 3500metres, by 8am we are on the road to Litang!!

Monday 4th October.......158441.....We see a long, long queue for diesel, luckily both our tanks are full.....It is now very cold, 8 degrees in car , we get our hats and gloves out.....

8.38am...4000metres up in the ice and snow on narrow windy roads with collapsed edges, sheer drops and lorries thundering towards us!!!! We are all feeling bad from the altitude, Angels lips have turned blue, which is very worrying. Up to 4412 then down a little.....we see horses, dogs, pot bellied black pigs, and cows all just wandering around on and off the roads, the children all stop and salute, even very tiny children, it's automatic!!!!

 12.40pm up again 4659m------1.55pm 4718m we stop for David and June to build a snowman---David is dizzy-----we all feel rough and very tired. It's not just the height, it's staying at it, for any length of time!! We all agree this is the hardest road yet!!

We see people chiselling the road by hand in order to fix it. It is constant, seeing people mending the roads, a never ending job, I suppose.

Eventually we arrive in Litang which is one of the highest cities in China (or the world?) at over 4000m......

We find a hotel, and we get the executive suite. Two double bedrooms and two bathrooms, a sitting area, with large flat screen. Seperate tv's in the bedrooms, not bad for £88 for all 8 of us......how different things can be, the toilets are good too!!!! Hurray!!!!

Tuesday 5th October.......158557.......Off at 10.30am -- up and through a magnificent , glacial valley. Up to 4696 - this is a killer of a mountain.....up to 5000 and up again through beautiful valleys, it's stunning, unmatched, and I feel so privileged to be seeing all this. Fingers crossed our bodies can cope. I'm sure they will!!

1pm back down to 4000--- June is feeling poorly. Alan keeps stopping for photos, he seems to be in no rush to get lower. There is black smoke from the Landrovers due to lack of oxygen, not just us humans suffering......

There are no barriers at the sides of the roads, just sheer drops. Back up to 5000..down to 4720....June is really ill now,,, Alan stops for more photos. The colours are stunning reds and oranges, we see people picking tea, wearing the typical Chinese hats with the baskets on their backs, as seen in photos and films!!!

Going down our brakes start to cook. We stop and the local children just appear, they are perhaps 6 to 8 years old with filthy faces and runny noses and tatty clothes. They look so happy with big smiles, which go even larger when we give them a bag of Smarties. Darren passes the sweets to them and they grab at his hand and scratch him, like hungry puppies with bones!!!

A&A stop and turn around to find us just as we are setting off again, so they turn around again to follow us. This means that, unknowingly, they have driven past the local police station 3 times, and they become curious. A policeman stops us and tells us we now have to go to the station and register, we know this is wrong and tell him so -- after a while he just gives up.

We find a hotel, half way to Shangri la----Darren and Agnes speak to an English speaking lady and explain that we have driven here, her answer is "Are you sure?" Love it!

Wednesday 6th October....158669......Last night we all felt rough with headaches, but seem ok today. Driving on cliff roads we see people sweeping the road, must be jobs for all, we think?

We are in the Sichuan province on the South Tibetan pass, road number the S2107, (the north side is said to be worse--how?) This is known to be the most dangerous road in the world and we agree!!! We are on a single track covered with snow, we are in the clouds and can hardly see the road ahead. Still high at 4337m. We stop because we see there are cars ahead. A lorry has gone over the edge of the road, and is wrapped around the trees on the steep slope. It obviously happened quite a while ago because there are two cranes attempting to move it. We have no information as to what happened, but at least in wasn't a sheer drop at that point, perhaps the driver may have escaped death. After an hour or so the cranes drivers give up, the road is too narrow and too crumbly, as they try to lift the lorry the cranes start to move as the road gives way underneath them. They pack up and move away. The cars try to pass both ways, all risking the same fate as the lorry---stupid--eventually they sort themselves out and we continue into the Yunnan province where the roads change to tarmac.....

We all agree that the S2107 would make a great Top Gear challenge!!!!

We drive on, then stop when we see a cyclist struggling up the hill. His name is Martino , from Italy, and he is a pizza chef. The bike goes on the roof of the Landy, Beverley jumps in the back with me, whilst Martino hops into the front, with his gear. We all drive into Shagri la looking for a decent hotel and a good pizza. The hotel is fine and opposite a place called Helens pizza......just what the doctor ordered!!!!!!!

Thursday 7th October....Day off at hotel........,

Friday 8th October....158791.......Breakfast at Helens pizza---12pm off---pouring with rain and cold. We pass colossal bamboo plants, (they should feed a few pandas), and many attractive tall pink and white flowers everywhere....

1.30pm and we arrive at the town of Tiger Leaping Gorge. We are informed that we are not allowed to drive to the gorge. It is 25k we could go on the bus, which takes an hour and a half each way, or with local guide, we decide to give it a miss, time is tight.

2.45pm We cross the Yangsy river, then we find a hotel.....

Saturday 9th.........Spend the day walking around Dali town----shops and shops and shops and pizza hut, very pretty and a Unesco sight, just so touristy.

Sunday 10th....158891........on the road again, we see rice fields, the peoples' faces are changing again......

Monday 11th.....158981.........12.30pm on road, suddenly it looks like the botanical gardens, the plants are massive, and there are (what I think) huge alo vera plants everywhere......

Tuesday 12th........159154.........10.20am off...it's hot--very hot--blue skies---the scenery looks unreal but it is real, it is jungle!!!!

Angel tells us the road we need to take is "a bit broken" in fact it is still being built. It's thick sticky mud---single track with two way traffic and land slides. By 3pm we have managed 46 miles. The road is being built by hand, there is some big machinery, but there are many people, including women and children. They are mixing cement by hand and using wheelbarrows to move rocks. The mud is so thick cars and buses keep getting stuck.

Alan decides there is no-one else to rescue this one particular bus, so we spend hours rescuing it. I can smell his Landy clutch burning. The locals find this very entertaining, they sit at the side of the road giggling and pointing. I can guess that they are asking "why is this man in such a rush to move the bus, usually we wait till the next day". It starts to go dark and it's raining. I have to admit I am getting very annoyed. Alan is putting us all at risk, his Landrover was never properly prepared for this trip and we now have to drive in the pitch black, in thick slippy mud, with sheer drops that we cannot see, to find a place to park for the night.

We find a pitch at the side of the road, where it suddenly widens out. The banks at the side of us are really steep and high, but there are many trees, which should stop a landslide, we are very lucky, I think, to find this!!!!! We see another 3ft snake slithering away!!! We set our two tents up, me, Beverley and June in one, Agnes, Angel and David in the other. Darren and Alan end up in pop up tents on the floor. The mud is everywhere, what will the inside of these tents look like in the morning? Who cares, they are warm and dry for tonight. This type of camping is not in the government rules, but we have no choice.

Wednesday 13th.....159217.....Yesterday we managed 63 miles in ten hours........this morning 10k in 40 minutes.......found a stretch of tarmac, nice while it lasted.

A&A have a problem--- ooh what a surprise!! - the clutch has gone!!!! We tow them to a hotel......

Thursday 14th October.....159325.......Our exit day for China is the 16th and we need to tow A&A 300k, we drive to the toll road but they refuse us entry---not allowed to tow. The other road could be mud all the way??? Angel organises a transporter, we drive back to hotel to wait for it.. should arrive at 3pm. It costs A & A £300 for the journey. 5.30pm the transporter arrives, me and Agnes get in the cab while everyone else squashes into James. After a very uncomfortable five and a half hours, we arrive at the border.

Happily, Angel finds us all a nice clean hotel. She has been exceptional throughout the whole journey. Many times she has entered hotels with her student card and booked us all in, once we are seen, as foreigners, the prices leap, but Angel argues on our behalf. She has taken us to so many places, each time saving us money, on entry into attractions and in restaurants. Without a doubt, she has paid for herself, this was her first journey away from home. I hope she has enjoyed our company as much as we have hers.

Friday 15th October...159492....To border 1km----Angel has no idea what we have to do, a very excited man arrives, on a motorbike, and Angel translates that he demands everyone must go to the police station immediately. It is going to close in half an hour and will not re-open until Monday. We cannot leave China without going there......so we rush like crazy people to get there on time. It's ok...it turns out not to be a a police station, but the border crossing. Everyone is very pleasant and relaxed, and it is open until 5.30pm.

We pass straight through China customs, which is a beautiful place, clean and tidy inside and surrounded by the most gorgeous gardens with seating areas. We say bye bye to Angel, promising to keep in touch.

Next we pass straight through Laos customs, no problems, we buy car insurance for a month for £35. No pretty gardens here but everyone is very friendly, with lots of smiling faces. We read up on the local wildlife, it includes wild elephants, jackals, bears, leopards, tigers and a rare dolphin called an Irrawaddy.

Again, as in China, no off road camping. Not government ruling, just the fact that Laos is full of un-exploded bombs dropped, I believe, by the Americans – I must read up on this!

As we drive Beverley points out that all the houses are on stilts. Why is the question-does it flood here, or is it the wildlife?

We, again, begin to tow A & A,--- travellers will always help other travellers, but I can't help thinking that this was self inflicted by Alan trying to be a hero. Our car was correctly prepped for this journey, but we did not take into account towing over 3 tons over mountain roads, will poor old James be up to this challenge, it's an awful lot to ask.

We tow A&A to Oudomxay, the first big town, where we meet Chrissy and Colin, who have also driven here from England, on their way to Australia. They arrived here yesterday, they tell us about a guest house/hotel, it is very clean, very pretty has a covered area outside with table and chairs, and a car park big enough for us all---perfect. We book in for 3 nights, at last we don't have to rush anywhere!!!!

Saturday 16th October....Lazy day, walked around town, relaxing with Beverley reading J.K Rowling to me--superb..............

Sunday 17th October......A&A have been sorting out what to do with their car, we think they might be able to get a clutch from Vientiane, the capital, they will have to wait till Monday to find out. I think they are very fortunate, as Darren has offered to fit the clutch for them.

Colin and Chrissy have a transit van , named Miranda, which Colin drives from his wheelchair, following a spinal cord injury. The van needs a starter motor amongst other things, they hope to get one sent here and (again Darren has volunteered to fit it). I think we may be here for a while. That suits me, as the company we are keeping at the moment is most enjoyable.

This morning, we went for breakfast at the local eatery, and saw a lady selling dried animal legs and a dead Chinese ferret badger,(we looked it up on google images) it seems they do hunting here, as well as rearing animals......

Monday 18th October.........Quiet day, we met a couple who have opened a school here, she is from Lao and he from America, they invite us to visit the school.

Tuesday 19th October.....Nobody here rushes to do anything, they even drive slowly, the people are very friendly and smile all the time. Laos Peoples Democratic Republic (LPDR) is referred to as Laos Please Don't Rush.

We meet students on their way to evening school, where they are learning English, they invite us to join them, and along with two guys from Israel, whom we have acquainted, we follow them. It is a very crowded room, full of students of all ages, they all seem very happy and we are made very welcome. We are introduced as the 'native English people' we are given microphones and asked heaps of questions, it was really good fun!!!!

Wednesday 20th October.....Hot!!!! Visited local museum - boring.....

21st to 24th....walked up to airport---5 minute walk--to see if the car parts that A&A ordered, might have arrived---no. So we went for a meal--on the menu it offered fried skin, we gave that a miss!! On the street you can buy deep fried frog or rat, the rat complete with ribs and huge teeth.

We had our first tropical rain storm, very heavy rain, thunder and lightning, but warm---- we went and stood in it till we were soaked---very refreshing!!!!!!

25th October. The car parts arrive for A&A, and Darren changes the clutch and brakes, with Alan helping, all fixed, hurray!!!! Alan thanks Darren for all his hard work, he is really pleased to have his Landy back. Agnes thanks Darren by telling him she thinks he is an idiot, and very stupid to have done the work, as he could of got hurt. I guess she has a point , but she could of been less insulting.

 Colin and Chrissy have gone on ahead to Vientiane, where they have parts waiting. Darren managed to persuade Miranda to start for them.

Tuesday 26th October............159553.....Off at 11.15, the guest house owners give us a little wooden pot as a gift, I shall keep it safe.

Up the mountain roads again, it's good to be moving!! The jungle is very thick and we can hear the insect drone over the sound of James' engine. We see many tracks at the side of the road, going into the jungle, some begin with wooden step ladders, as the bank is so steep. In parts there has been logging, we are told it's usually done illegally. Vast areas have gone and we can see where it has caused landslides.....we pass through many villages which belong to different hill tribes, some are so beautiful and the flowers are gorgeous, others are drab and sad.

We arrive at Luang Probang, it's very touristy and we soon find a great guesthouse with a balcony and tv etc... about £9 per room. In the evening we go to the night market, it's full of stalls selling hand- made jewellery and clothes, and of course T.shirts. We buy trousers for Darren--very hippy==two beautiful dresses for Beverley and some jewellery and a few T.shirts, not that we need them. I'm also running out of space in the car to put them all!!!!!

Wednesday 27th October.....strolled around town, took pictures of the river Mekong.......

Thursday 28th October.....11.30am we leave--after Darren has had a bacon and egg breakfast, the food is getting better and better......We have left A&A, they are going on elephant rides and visiting the waterfall. On asking Beverley if she would like to ride an elephant she replied "why would I want to do that?" and seeing the waterfall "seen one before" . So we're off to Vientiane, --we will do the elephants, but further on down.

The currency here is the kip, there are 12.500 kip to £1-----today in my purse I have £80, therefore I am a millionaire!!!!

Up mountain roads through villages, we see a tiny boy playing in a puddle, another playing with a tyre and a man weaving a basket. The people take no notice of us at all, they are all so cool, and relaxed. There are people cutting the border of the jungle at the edge of the road so there is a grass verge. A lot of the houses are made from grasses or reeds which are woven together. Driving through one village we accidently drive over a dog, but he is so tiny he comes out the back untouched!!!! We see many animals such as chickens, ducks, geese, pigs, water buffalos, dogs and cats. The only wild things we have seen are lizards, and insects, apart from one huge spider I saw, running up a wall, and a black and white one, that had its web across the pavement, it was attacked by a wasp and fell to the floor, as we watched it a local man came up and warned us that one bite would kill you, we took a step back.

The jungle scenery is breathtaking, I cannot properly describe it. I've seen it on tv and read about It, but being here is different it's incredible!!!

We arrive at Vangvieng--half way to the capital. There are dozens of guest houses, me and Beverley try five but they are all damp and dirty. It is starting to go dark and we might not be able to find anywhere to camp, so we try another guesthouse, this last one is clean and there is a parking pitch, all for £8 a night, that will do. Then we go and have food, Beverley gets her pizza, and it's delicious, Darren has steak, also delicious. Back to the guesthouse to watch English tv, something very comforting about listening to your own language,,,,,then sleep........

Friday 29th October.......159789.....Up and out for 8.30am.

Drivers here are also calm, each time we drive up behind a lorry they pull over and wave us past!!!

After a couple of hours the landscape changes, we leave the mountains and it becomes flat and open. We pass a cyclist and stop to chat, his name is Xavier from France, he's a bit behind schedule so we give him a lift, with the bike on top of the tents. We arrive at Vientiane and bump into Chrissy and Colin, we arrange to meet at Sticky Fingers bar with Xavier....they introduce us to their friends Katrina and John who live here in the capital. It was a very enjoyable evening with such good company.

We find a good guesthouse called Orchid, it has a patio roof where we can watch the busy road with the street vendors and it overlooks the Mekong river--perfect.....

Saturday 30th....Very hot!!! We see a 3 wheeled tuk tuk with a big sign saying 4 wheel drive.....Almost next door to the guesthouse is a mini-mart and when we walked in I thought I'd gone to heaven, it sells cheeses, something we have not had for months and Beverley finds Vegemite, the marmite ran out ages ago!!!!

Me and Beverley spend time on the patio, she reads to me and I plait her hair, while Darren is working on the Landy, we can see him across the road. He works on the front suspension bushes and finds a badly worn track rod end--it has only done 20,000 miles!!

We call in at the Land Rover showroom , they show us a brand new defender, the import tax on it is 30,000 dollars, only 9,000 on the pick up, now I know why there are so many pick ups. This supposedly poor country is jammed with very expensive cars, every other car is a Hilux!!!

Saturday 31st October........Halloween, this time last year we were in deep snow!! Beverley and I remember being back in Villajou, walking back to our house in the dark, creepy!

We took a drive around the town, it is growing really fast, all along the river bank it is being turned into gardens and pathways. We saw one huge statue being put into place, it will be really beautiful when finished, and no doubt a huge tourist attraction.

The sad part is that, this huge area was home to countless people who have just been moved off. We see some of them walking around the town begging. I read in the guide book that there is no net for the poor or displaced people and that the government follow the belief that the poor people deserve to be poor to be punished for the bad they have done in their past lives.

We go to Katrina and Johns house for a party and we meet some very interesting and lovely people. They have a huge swimming pool and invite us to use it...by the side of the pool is a bbq made from an unexploded bomb, John explains to us that this is his job, working with the unexploded bombs, not building bbq's.

Monday 1st November......Katrina and John very kindly said we could visit their house to work on our car, and so we do. Not being of any use to Darren, me and Beverley sit by the pool and read, we watch as the pool is cleaned and the chlorine put in, so no swimming today. On the evening we go to the Italian restaurant, can pizza really be this good? Exceptional!

Tuesday 2nd November......Darren takes the Landy to the Ford garage to get the oil and filter changed. It was my idea, because of the mess involved changing the oil----never again----they wanted 248 dollars for an easy job, and Darren had to show them where the filter was. Darren argued them down to 190 dollars. While he was there he finds out that they hadn't started work on Colin and Chrissys car, although it had been there for over a week.

We go back to Katrina and Johns and catch up with Colin and Chrissy, who are staying there. This time me and Beverley had a swim, it was wonderful, we really enjoyed it!!!

We arrange to meet up that evening for a meal.

In the afternoon we visit COPE, (Cooperative Orthotic and Prosthetic Enterprise). They deal with the injured from the unexploded bombs. They have a wheelchair factory and make prosthetic limbs plus a great deal more. I read, that although Laos was not involved in the Vietnam war, it is the most bombed country in the world. It was bombed every day for 9 years, one plane load every eight minutes, by the U.S. pilots attempting to bomb the Ho Chi Minh trail. As Laos was not actually in the war, there were no rules to follow, so the U.S could continue bombing, it became known as the secret war. Between 1964 and 1973 around 2 million tons were dropped, and about a third of these failed to explode. No matter how hard people like John work, there are still thousands of bombs out there just waiting for someone, perhaps a child playing, or a farmer digging, it happens all the time, some say as often as every other day, someone is injured or killed.!!!

Have a good meal with Chrissy, Colin, Xavier....

Wednesday 3rd November........159939......We give our jerry cans to John as a thank you, sounds crazy but he did really want them. We say our goodbyes to Colin and Chrissy and start to follow the Mekong down south.

We drive into National park to a waterfall called Tai Say, we walk across a very dodgy wooden bridge and follow a path through the jungle, it doesn't go far, to some eye-catching huge rocks and pools. We cook some noodles, I wonder how many families have stopped here to cook noodles in the jungle. I think I can say we are the first, but you never know, and then we drive on.

We find a hotel down a side street it's ok and costs just £7.50, we have a picnic in the room and watch a bit of telly........

Thursday 4th November.......160051......off at 9.30am, we turn off the main road and head towards Konglor to see the famous cave...we find an eco-lodge where we can have a room for £4, it only has one big bed, but we decide it's ok just for one night....we meet lots of travellers as they arrive....Macey from Canada---Kaitlin from U.S.----Rico from Germany-----Lisa and Stew from Scotland----Fred and Celine from France---we all start telling our stories while we have a meal and a beer......

Friday 5th November........160171....Lisa, Stew, Celine and Fred have left...the rest of us go to the cave, which is a 7and a half km tunnel with a river running through. Climbing into long boats---with an outboard motor---- and then entering a pitch black tunnel is really scary for me at first. We stop and visit a cave with stalactites, this part is lit, then back into boats—here the only light being the boatsmans torch---starting to enjoy it now---Beverley and Darren think it's great. We have to climb out and they carry the boats over rocks and then off we go again. We come out of the tunnel and take a break, the return journey being special for me, as now I am getting real pleasure from the trip, not being cooied anymore.

After this we leave to go to Lak Sao which is part of the Ho Chi Min trail----Macey and Kaitlin were going by tuktuk, but Rico has a spare seat on his motorbike and we also have one -so we all set off together. We have totally run out of money and Kaitlin has to pay the road toll for us, only 40 pence but if you haven't got it!!!!! Lesson learnt, thanks Kaitlin.

We leave them at the bus station and drive on down, going south again. This road is appalling ---back to no tarmac---dirt and pot holes, at one point we slide and the Landy very nearly tips over.

We arrive in the dark at a travel lodge, they do not have a room, but they let us put the tent up in the grounds, and we can use the toilets and restaurant, perfect. Strolling to the restaurant to order a meal and who is sitting there- Lisa, Stew, Celine and Fred!!!

Saturday 6th November..........Off at 8am. We are passing acres of sugar beet. Arrive and spend the day in Savannakhet---it's a poor place, the whole town needs a visit from the dulux dog. It is described as historic, which obviously it is, but the words old and worn out jump to mind. We find a guest house down a quiet road with good parking for James.

Getting dark and we head for the Starlight restaurant, the sign read Starlihgt. It was described as having an extensive western menu, this consisted of chips bread and egg, which Beverley had with rice, Darren had fries and pork and I had veg and noodle, it was edible and not poisonous, say no more!

Sunday 7th November......160389..........Drove out of town to find a temple where the monkeys are all over you, sounds like fun. The map is less than useless and we cannot find the place, never mind. We drive back to town and visit the market. Me and Darren find new sandals. We see masses of frogs with their back legs speared together so they cannot jump out of the dish. They are waiting to be deep fried, I contemplate over a horrific thought, do they know. I take into account that they must know the sound of their kin screaming, so the answer is yes, I just hope they don't suffer fear!

Stopped at the river to have a beer--that is a beer Lao, I read that it's government owned,and they have about 90% of the market here. Then we spot the Mekong restaurant---pizza, steaks, our mouths are watering. Followed by an incredible sight --- Lisa and Stew arrive on a motorbike. They join us for a beer, and we arrange to go to a French restaurant in the evening. Plenty of chatting and beer Lao, a very enjoyable evening!!!!!!

Monday 8th November..........160474........Up at 9am, (slight head-ache) sitting outside at the guesthouse, drinking green tea and writing this. It is 32degrees in the shade with a nice breeze, what a life.

We drive off and buy fresh pineapple and tiny oranges still on the branch, lovely breakfast, thinking to myself, could it get any better?

We pass the temple with the monkeys but we're not in the mood now.

We arrive at Pakse, and find a cheap hotel, it's ok. The map states that there is a big shopping plaza, we tell each other not to hold our breath, we manage to find two boxes of Kellogs frosties, and a lovely top for Beverley, well at least we found something!!!!

Tuesday 9th November.......160622......We drive to the Bolaven plateau, we see waterfalls and visit a coffee plantation. Being the only coffee drinker, I had a cup, for the experience of sitting in a plantation and tasting the produce. It was good, but not really worth the four times the price of a normal local coffee, which I'm sure is the same, but I've done it!

In the evening we go for an Indian meal, it was perfect---Darren had prawn curry and we also shared pakora and samosa, garlic nan bread, Beverley and me shared a spicy chick pea curry. As we sat there, ingesting all the diverse tastes, I saw two rats running up the wall. It reminded me of Birmingham, we had seen many a rat in some (not all) of the Indian restaurants, the difference being the rats in Birmingham were twice the size. With our tummies full, wo buy some more films at 25p each, and go back to our room.

Wednesday 10th November.......160737........10am and we are going south 120km to Si Phan Don---four thousand islands. This is where the Mekong is at its widest, there is a car ferry to Don Khong, the biggest island, which is 18km long and 8km wide.

We find the ferry it is tiny, just 4 cars at a time, we have no problems. Soon we arrive and find a beautiful guest house, we go for a walk and bump into Lisa and Stew, we share a beer and then another.....................

Thursday 11th November........We move to the next guest house,(after a tip-off) it is just as nice but half the price. Today we drive around the island, we see five schools, we have never seen so many children as there are in Laos.

We find out we have just missed Xavier, he left on Tuesday, I am sitting on a balcony overlooking the Mekong as I write this, it is very hot and very ,very beautiful. Tomorrow we leave for Cambodia!!!!!!

Friday 12th November.......160843......There is nowhere around where we can get cash, so we decide to drive back to Pakse it's 120km but necessary.

Doing the final research on Cambodia, I find in small print, that the international driving license is not enough, we will also need a local license. Apparently it is very easy to arrange in Phnom Penn or Siem Reap, when you fly in, but that's no good to us!!!! Shall we risk it and just go? After being told by many travellers that the police in Cambodia are very corrupt, we decide not to go-----so change of plan we head for Thailand.............by 12.30pm we are driving to the border crossing.

The custom official is very friendly, but we have a problem. He tells us that we are the first French registered car to enter at this crossing. He is amazed at how we have arrived here, he asks us if we have arrived by sea, coming from a land locked country this is unlikely. The computer will not accept our number plate, but he seems determined, and after about half an hour he has sorted it, what a nice man! As we are waiting we meet a group of people who work in Laos, they are waiting to cross the border to do their shopping at Tesco. Naturally we ask for directions---oooh Tesco!!!!!!

We are stamped into Thailand---no visa needed, we have 15 days and for some strange reason can only insure the car for 9 days------we decide to travel north west and go to Chiang Mai first---here (we believe) we can extend our visas. It is the year 2453. We drive straight to Tesco. Tesco sliced bread, cheese---cheese sandwich it's so, so good-----Beverley chooses fresh brocolli, red pepper, a twix and a Tesco jelly---heaven!!!

Saturday 13th November........161006....9am......Yasothon to Roi Et. 3.30pm arrive at Khon Kaen, the roads are perfect. We see remnants of the flooding, some houses are still under water---it is 36 degrees in the shade. We find the Roma hotel, pretty comfortable, and it has signs for wifi, but it won't work for us!!!!

In the evening we are sitting outside at a restaurant eating, when an elephant wanders past, brilliant!!!!

Sunday 14th November........We spent the day in town---so hot!! We buy new pc games for Beverley, but they don't work. Then, Darren remembers the new games for her nintendo that Stew and Lisa gave us, yes they work! In the evening we see the elephant again, this time Beverley and Darren go over and fuss and feed it, I stayed at the table to watch our things, as we are back in a city. Then it's back to hotel to watch the Formula one race......

Monday 15th November......161175......10.30am on road. Travelling through nature reserves, this is exceptional. Every few km there is a sign for `Caution elephant crossing`, shame we didn't actually see one crossing, but we could ooc evidence of where they had. Fantastic thick dark jungle, imagine what else is living in there!

We drive to Lom Sak to Phitsanulok to Sukhothai----we are looking for somewhere special to stop for Beverleys birthday tomorrow. Perhaps a luxury hotel, we see a sign for a guest house with swimming pool so we decide to check it out. It is beautiful, a proper holiday place, flowers everywhere, we rent a bungalow---3 beds, lovely clean shower, t.v. wifi and best of all the pool, we book in for two nights,

Tuesday 16th November.......I am sitting on the porch writing this while Beverley and Darren are watching The Big Bang Theory, we have been swimming and it's a perfect day! We bought cakes to celebrate, as usual we don't want to eat them, just too sweet for us. We take them to the cafe and offer them around to the other guests, they like them, and all wish Beverley a happy birthday.

Wednesday 17th. 161385.......We went to see the local historical site, it was just so hot, 39 in the car. A quick walk around is all we managed, interesting, lots of tombs and old remnants.

I seem to be accident prone today. I have dropped a glass jar full of chocolate spread. I had a biting insect down the front of my swimming costume whilst in the water, on jumping out of the pool I trod on a gigantic ant, who stung me with his acid, boy did that make me hop. Then I slipped on the tiled floor, went down fast with a crash, hitting my back and elbow on the stone step, scared Beverley, how I didn't break something I don't know, must be tough. Darren copied me and slipped, luckily he managed to grab the rail and stop himself. Finishing off, I got bitten twice by some sort of huge grotesque house fly.

Thursday 18th November 2010.......161403.............10am start heading for Lampang. Arrive and follow the map to the elephant camp. The map is wrong, we have wasted about 80 miles, never mind. We double check that it's not us, no, the map has the camp on the wrong road.... Eventually we find it, on the road to Chang Mai, the way we were going in the first place, it's 4.30pm and it's closed for today! There is a sign that states that this is also a resort, so we drive in. Stop and say hello to a baby elephant and fed him some bananas, his keeper points us to the right way. What a picturesque sight – wooden bungalows in the middle of the jungle with huge elephants roaming around. We find the reception where we are warmly welcomed, by a gentleman who seems to be all alone. He advises us to just stand still to watch the elephants, not to get too close as they will most likely kill us if we annoy them, we hear him! We are given a bungalow, which is just wonderful, and invited to the restaurant. He cooks us a lovely meal and gives us tickets to enter the elephant show tomorrow.

Friday 19th… 161621….Sitting on the balcony drinking green tea. The view couldn't be more beautiful. 9.30 off to the elephant show, we watch them painting, playing instruments and moving logs, then we fed them with sugar cane. At last we take our elephant ride, around the grounds, very enjoyable.

11.30am and we're off to the beautiful walled city of Chaing Mai

20th to 26th November.....Reached Chang Mai and found a very pleasant guest house. We have tried and tried to buy car insurance, but it's ridiculous, nobody wants to insure us.

We have found a great looking guitar, we buy it for a late birthday present for Beverley, the last one fell of the trailer, somewhere in Europe and shattered.

We are having trouble with the gear box in James. When we were towing A&A through the mountain roads, their brakes failed and the only way for them to stop was to run into the back of us. Well poor old James is now showing the bruises, and with the insurance running out, we have decided to cut across and head back to Laos.

Saturday 27th November.....162345......We arrive in Vientiane and try to find an apartment with somewhere to work on the car, no luck, can't find anything suitable, so we drive up to see Katrina and John to ask If we can use their drive and Johns welder. We are greeted by Katrina, who not only agrees to the use of the drive, but invites us to stay in the house, a little later John arrives home and greets us with a big smile.

These people are just so generous and kind!!!! They have a gorgeous, almost two year old little boy, named Casper, and two lovely black labs. Quite unexpected they also cook dinner for us, all this from people who hardly know us.....

Sunday and Monday.. 28-29th Darren starts work on James, he takes off the fuel and water tanks. There is nothing me and Beverley can do to help so, we swim in the pool.

We go into town and hire 3 push bikes, Beverley is shaking, she has never ridden a bike on a busy road before, she is brilliant!!!

Darren takes off the transfer box and the gear box. He doesn't have all the correct tools and after hours of fighting to get inside the gear box he decides to order a new (recon) from England.

Tuesday... 30th ..Swim---cycle to town....Darren cycles for miles to find the steel for the welding.....there is a lot to do.....he had requested Foley's to do this before we started our journey, when the extra tanks were being fitted, but they did not do it!!!! Colin and Chrissy arrive back from Singapore, where they had been for a hospital visit,.....they are still awaiting news on their car........surprised to see us!!!

December

Wednesday...Thursday... 1st and 2nd Darren does the welding and we do the swimming!!

Friday. 3rd ..We move into hotel, quite close about 5=10 mins on bikes, Katrina is off to Cambodia for the weekend and we really have stayed a long time. Me and Beverley cycle around Vientiane to find a suitable Christmas present for Casper. We find a toy shop and buy him a lego set, hopefully he will love it. We say a big thankyou and we move out of the house, but of course are still working on the drive, and we can still use the pool!!

Saturday 4th Darren has finished the welding, and painted over it all, thanks to John who gave us a pot of blue gloss.

Sunday 5th Two fuel tanks back in, it was a real hard slog for Darren to get them back in, at least I managed to be a bit useful today and helped him a bit.....

Monday 6th December....water tank back in, now we are waiting for news on the gearbox, the tracker for the parcel says it has arrived, so we hope to pick up today...

Tuesday 7th December........Darren cycles to the TNT office to be told that the gear box is sitting at customs awaiting collection and import tax payment, which could be as much as 2 to 300 pounds..... John to the rescue again, we borrow his car (with diplomatic number plates) and arrive at customs. The parcel has a U.N. address (Johns') so there is no tax to pay, just a £4 handling charge

Darren sets to work and puts the gearbox in and then the transfer box, ----- it looks so easy in writing, but I bet there are not many people who could do what Darren has done, with-out a winch or half the correct tools, and just me to help ------ all done---brilliant!!!!! Just the cleaning up to do tomorrow.......

Wednesday 8th December.......We drive to the petrol station and fill up, then to the Thai embassy for our next visas. We notice the petrol is pouring out underneath the Landy, this is not what we wanted. The embassy is closed and tomorrow is a holiday, so we decide not to bother.

Back to John and Katrinas'......draining the 100 litres of diesel out into various buckets, and the jerry cans that we gave to John and now have to borrow back. Darren takes the tank out again and finds a leak on the seal. He uses 'petro patch' - this was given to him by the lads who drove the ambulance to Mongolia, it's a quick fix, but it works, then we clean up.........................Tonight we are going for a meal with John, Katrina, Chrissy and Colin, to say bye and thank them for all their kindness...............................

Thursday 9th.......162464.......Great meal last night---Italian restaurant, pizza.........

We have loved Vientiane, we have eaten snake eggs and birthday cake and drank beer Lao with the locals and have been given so much help, what could have been a disaster has been a great time!!!!!!!

We drive 22km to the Lao – Thai friendship bridge and arrive at customs at 1.30pm, half an hour later we are through with a 14day visa and 30 days car insurance.

Now south to Bangkok......

We stop for the night at Khon Kaen and go to the same Roma hotel that we used last time we were here, on our way north to Chiang Mai....we watch more new videos.....Star Trek and Black Books.........

Friday 10th......162588.....We see a sign 'Happy New Year 2554' We are heading for Nakhon Ratchasima (aka Khorat) population 2.2 million, it's the second biggest city in Thailand---should break us in for Bangkok, our book says it doesn't have much going for it!

 We stop at Tesco and buy lots of treats, fresh bread, bags of salad, oranges......... We find the Thai hotel - it's fine, we eat on the street and then make our own garlic bread with our toaster in our room, and watch Top Gear videos........

Saturday 11th December.......162697......off at 11.15am, slow start due to watching an hour of Top Gear.

3pm Bangkok---we stop at Tesco to use the toilet and me and Beverley are surprised to find that the toilet paper they supply is old newspapers ripped up, and put in a basket attached to the wall, (we supplied our own) it's not how you think of Tesco!!!

Darren spots a hotel--The Golden Horse, it has a car park with security, the rooms have everything and they are clean, at £21 a night it is better than we thought it would be. This is central Bangkok!!!!!

Sunday 12th ....so so hot......we go to the famous Khao San road, it is very, very busy and just full of backpackers. It seems a lot cleaner than last time we were here, which was quite a few years ago!! You can buy any kind of forged document you want, Beverley is offered an International driving licence and a new passport!!!!! We see the advertising for diving on the island of Ko Tao---looks brilliant---will need to extend our visa!!!

Monday 13th.....we set off to immigration for our visas. We need to turn right and therefore drive into the right hand turn lane. For some reason this seems to upset a policeman who pulls us out of the lane and makes us park up. He explained to us that if we go into that lane we have to turn right---yes seems obvious to us--then he goes onto explain that this is going to cost us 400 baht, about £8, or a visit to the police station. We agree on the visit to the station, he then sends us on our way, looking very disappointed!!!! This was really annoying as it had taken us ages to find a right hand turn, and now we have to start again!

At immigration we are told this is the wrong office for visas. So it's off to the British Embassy for a different address. The Embassy inform us that we will need a letter from them to obtain the visa, and to come back in the morning.

Tuesday 14th December......Last night we atc on the street, we had white chicken and rice, very tasty. The other choice was grilled pig penis!!!

Back to the Embassy and there is no-where for us to park, and we are told you cannot park outside the Embassy. Darren parks opposite in a car park . After a lot of messing around we eventually get inside at 8.30am.

I explained about coming back for the letter, as instructed, to be told that this was an utter load of rubbish. I did not need a letter, but I could have one if I wanted to pay £40, I declined! Then I was given the new address for immigration. Unfortunately the lady behind the counter decided she wanted to explain to us how to get there. I say unfortunately because, she began with a detailed description on how to leave the car park. At this point Darren had to leave the office and wait outside, I stood there smiling like a moron, not wanting to upset an official person in a strange country. Apart from gaining the address, which they could have given us yesterday, we had wasted hours.

It turned out that the new address was miles away, so we returned to the hotel. We asked the tuktuk drivers, they said it would be better to go by boat and it would take a couple of hours. Then we asked at the hotel reception, an English speaking lady explained to us how to get there by car. It would probably take us until lunch time to get there, at which point they would close for the day, so that was now a whole day wasted, thankyou British Embassy!!!! We decide not to bother and head for Phuket where we can get visas on the way.......

Wednesday 15th December.....162885.........On leaving Bangkok the Kings car pulls along side us, we thought he had come to say bye to us personally--but he wasn't there, just his driver having a look at us. Thanks to Darren and his great sense of direction, we are out of the city by 10.30am, heading towards Samut Sarhon, just one hour after setting off....brilliant!! At 12.30pm we are at Cha-am in the gulf of Thailand. We drive to a beach-it seems to be private, with a security guard, he tells us it's ok and to have a swim. The sea is so warm and the sand so white-love it.

We continue on to Prachuap Khiri Khan, a very pretty sea-side town. At the north end of the town is Khao Chang Krajon, which means mirror tunnel mountain. There are hundreds of monkeys, some of which immediately jump onto our car. There is a lady selling food for them, Beverley buys a bag and has it snatched out of her hand in seconds. The young monkeys are quite sweet, but the adults are aggressive and scary, and they all look a bit manky with horrible growths.

Further down the coast we find a beautiful beach with views across the sea to rocky islands, it's stunning. Here we find a smashing guest house right on the beach, a large room, big enough for 4, with tv, fridge etc. £14 a night. We take another swim, just as the sun is setting, we are the only people here, the sea is so warm. Back at the guest house we meet two great ladies, Heather and her daughter Morgan, they are from Canada, we exchange e-mails....

Thursday 16th December......At midday, after Beverley eventually gets out of bed, we go for another swim, and on the beach Beverley collects some colourful mother of pearl shells. We go for a walk into town, (passing the monkeys), and eat on the street again. Afterwards we drive to the military base to see some other monkeys we have been told about. These are so different, they are black and grey with long tails and white around the eyes. They are so friendly, they hold our hands, these are very healthy, not aggressive at all. Many of them have the sweetest bright orange babies, what a wonderful sight! We sit with them for quite a while, us studying them and them us. At one point I sit under a branch to view them, yes I got peed on, silly me.

On the evening we go to Ann and Alans bar, we meet some Germans, Canadians, Finnish and English people, eat fish and chips and learn a lot about visas, a very entertaining friendly evening. Then it's back to guest house and as requested, I colour Beverleys' hair blond........looks great!

17th December.......Yesterday and through the night we have had storms and rain, the forecast says it will rain for the next ten days, will have to wait and see, seems ok today?

 More problems with James, now the alternator has stopped working. Darren dismantles it and starts off towards town. Walking past Alans bar he stops to say hello. Alan phones his Aussie friend Bob, who arrives on his motorbike and takes Darren straight to a mechanic who fixes the problem for £4. Again the kindness of people just shines, and we thought we might have to order a new alternator from England!!!

We go for a drive in the car and all is well. Beverley is reading and has nearly finished another book.

This evening we buy Bob a meal and a beer, at Alans bar, of course. Alan tells us that on Sunday he is going to Burma to renew his visa, and so are we, he explains it all to us, we might see him there.

Walking back to the guest house we have to pass many dogs that live wild here, it is sad to see, many of them are in really bad condition, and some are just nasty, I found a large stick on the beach and have taken to walking with this.

Saturday 18th December.....163132............10.20am off to Ranong. Tomorrow we are going to cross, by ferry to Kawthong, Burma---- Myanmar-----for 15 day visa. We find a guest house for the night, weather is still ok.....

Sunday 19th......163304......We arrive at the pier, the crossing is all arranged by the Andaman club. We pass through passport control, customs and onto a ferry, then onto a coach which takes us a short journey to a 5 star resort, where we have lunch, then back on the coach, ferry, back in Thailand for 1pm. We met Alan and Ann on the way back. Now we can say we've been to Burma but we don't think it really counts as a proper visit!!!!!

We have our 15day visa --off to Phuket.......

Driving down through Khao Lak , here was one of the worst affected areas in the 2004 tsunami. There is a policeboat 2km inland. There has been much preparation for the future, should there be a repeat episode, many signs showing the escape routes for earthquakes and tsunami---- scary!!!

We arrive on Phuket at 5pm and head for Kamala beach, from our research it should be quieter here than the main resorts, and have diving facilities.

Suddenly there is a very loud banging, followed by the horrible sound of metal on metal grinding. At this point I am convinced James is dead and something very big must have fallen off!!!!! Darren calmly pulls over and has a look underneath, he can't see anything.

We then drive until we see the sign 'rooms available' at a place called The Club, we check it out.....for £20 a night, we have tv fridge, large room - two beds- good bathroom, and it's all clean, plenty of storage room and tables, fan and aircon. Outside there is a balcony, with chairs, overlooking the small swimming pool, another huge pool is just a few yards away, plus a jacuzi. Believing it cannot get better, we discover that breakfast is included, we book in for 6 days, we are settled for Christmas, what a superb feeling. At reception we meet an Englishman called Sean, whilst chatting he tells us the beach is just 5-10 minute walk and the diving course can be booked just up the road. Minutes later Darren and Sean drive off on a motorbike and shortly return with everything booked.........

Monday 20th......Darren checks the car, it's the rear wheel flanges that are worn out----it's a lot better than we thought!!! At 1pm we are picked up to go to a resort, for Darren and Beverley to start their diving course,....we pick up books and videos, then come back and have a swim before going to the doctor for Darren to have the doc check out his asthma, the doctor signs him off as fit and just says to take care........

Tuesday 21st December.......8.20am back to resort. I sit in while Darren and Beverley do the classroom studies, then they get all geared up and off to huge-huge swimming pool for first dive, we are in a 5 star complex with a beautiful beach, not bad!

Wednesday 22nd December......Back to the resort for sea diving,.....they both gear up and set off, I wait on the beach, I find a shady corner with rock pools and hundreds of tiny hermit crabs. I see them returning and go and meet them.......they have completed their first sea dive together!!!! Then Beverley tells us that she did not like it, she says she has not enjoyed any of it and does not want to continue, ok it's not for everyone, she's had a good go and completed a sea dive. We inform the diving company and they return some of the money, tomorrow is the boat dive, we decide to all go together, but just Darren diving.......

Thursday 23rd December......we are picked up at 7.30am and taken to the pier, the boat can take 40 people but there are only about 20 and that includes the instructors. We are told that normally the boats are full at this time of year, but most of the customers are still stuck in the snow in England. We sail for about 3 hours, past beautiful islands, until we arrive at the dive sight, the first dive is done and then we have lunch, followed by a second dive, Darren is enjoying himself and is now qualified--again--after losing all his papers!!! Me and Beverley have a lovely day on the boat, we see thousands of fish as the water is so crystal clear, but today we have decided to stay dry.....a few more hours back to shore, another fantastic day!!!!!

Christmas eve.......the sun is back, it is so hot and only 8.30am, today we are going to the beach and swimming pool,,,,, when Beverley gets up! Darren is waiting for the man at the local garage to return, at about mid-morning, he is going to get the car fixed by having the flanges to the half shafts welded.

Christmas day, Saturday 25th December 2010..........We have a lazy morning. I was not able to find anything to wrap up for presents, except one teddy, whom we have named Miss Fwibble. I think waking up in this beautiful place is enough for us all.

To the white sand beach, it's a gorgeous day, clear blue skies, like a dream. The sea is warm and crystal clear, it has an aqua-marine tint and we can see so many beautiful fish, it's picture book!, We spend ages playing in the waves -- perfect---what a way to spend Christmas day. Then back to the hotel and the swimming pool......pizza for dinner.....then after a power cut we watch some 'Black books', and have a read in bed. Reflecting on our journey, wow, then fall asleep..........

Boxing day.........163518......10am -- packed and off to Krabi. We find a super bungalow to stay, it has everything, and James is parked just outside. We go to explore Ao Nang beach. It is spectacular, the sea is emerald green, there are limestone rocks with karst formations, outstanding views. After this it's back to the bungalow to watch some of the new Dr.Who series that we have saved specially for xmas.......

Monday 27th December.......10am packed and off to Trang. The peoples faces are changing again. I believe the main religion around here is Muslim, and there are loads of mosques.

We go to the beach but it is not clean, such a disappointment after the last few days. Off to Sutun, the beach here is the same but with 14 to 15 inch jelly fish, interesting to see, but that's all.

We leave for the town, for the night........driving into town we, again, hear the screeching sound of metal on metal . The welding on the flanges has failed, then Beverley notices that the half shaft is sticking out of the wheel by about 2 feet. We pull over, luckily she spotted this, we could easily have driven the half shaft into one of the many motorcyclists. Darren removes it and we drive on to a hotel----we are fortunate it is nice and clean===£11 a night, with a car park.....

Tuesday 28th......163845.........Darren goes to fix the car. He asks a local tuk-tuk driver if there is a local garage, oh yes he says, then claims the nearest is 270 km away. Naturally he offers to drive Darren there for a 'special price'!!! Darren drives off in James and finds a garage less than 1km away, surprise, surprise! He returns at midday, the weld looks stronger.

Off to town for some food, there is no western food here, obviously not on the tourist route.

12.20pm and the weld has broken again, that didn't last long! We drive back to the same garage to show them what has happened. Two guys, from the garage (we hope) drive off in James, we thought they were just going to park it. They say nothing and just drive away down the road, with our passports and everything we own in the world. This is one of those times when you have to smile and have trust in people. We stand and wait, a tropical rainstorm starts, it's fantastic to watch, there is so much water in such a short time. At 2.30 pm James returns with a new weld and everything intact, just as it should be.....

Wednesday 29th.......163863.....It's raining, we set off towards the Malaysian border. We cross at Kuandon over to Wang Kelian. This crossing is not mentioned in the guide book, so not many travellers pass this way. They have never seen a French registered car before, we are the first ever, yet another place in the record book for us!!!! They refuse to sell us any insurance and insist that our carnet de passage covers all, but of course it doesn't. As, what now seems to be usual, they have no idea of what they are doing. So they issue us a 90 day visa and send us on our way, rather pleased to see us, the strange problem, driving away.

2.15pm and the rain eventually stops. We are heading south looking for an ATM.....the people speak a little English and the skies are grey.

We find a pizza hut and we order, after a good half an hour the waiter comes back to take our order again, it's so frustrating. It becomes obvious that they do not want to serve us, whether they speak English or not, pointing at pictures of pizza is not hard to understand. We leave and go back to our room and have garlic and tomato on toast, who needs pizza!!!

Thursday 30th .....163955....... on our way to Butterworth we pass an enormous Tesco and massive shopping malls. There are literally hundreds of motorbikes, although there are only one or two people on them and most are wearing crash helmets. This makes a change from Thailand where we saw entire families on one bike including babies and dogs!!

We cross the huge Penang bridge and see dozens of high rise buildings across the water....we are aiming to go past George town to Batu Ferringi, our travel book says it has the best beach.

My impression of Malaysia is that it looks like it needs a good tidy up and a paint job. Everything looks old and worn out, and there is a lot of rubbish around, not a good start.

We go to an Indian restaurant and have the worst service, again. Darren refuses to pay the service charge, quite right, then he asks the owner if she can recommend a decent place to eat, not very pleasant, but she deserved it. Then we take a walk around the night market, (bit of a tradition now). It is made up of Chinese, Malay and Indian people. The smell is different from Thailand....

Friday 31st December 2010......164037.......We are just about to clock 40,000km!!!!

To Georgetown for breakfast/dinner, pizza hut again, but this time great service, we call in at Tesco for supplies and visit their toilet. it is one of the smelliest ever----shame on you Tesco. We visit the beach, supposed to be great, it's crap. So much for Batu Ferringi----back to hotel......then we go for another Indian meal. This place is lovely and the service is excellent!!! Really good to be recognised as people again and to know that all the bad service the other day was just bad luck.

We have an internet connection so we wish everyone in England a happy new year, then a bit of tv and sleep-------------

Saturday 1st January 2011.........164064.......11am off through palm tree plantations, jungle and mountains, it's hot, very humid and we are all stuck to our chairs. I have washing which I have been trying to dry, it has been blowing in the wind for hours but is still as damp as when it started. Black clouds appear, then monsoon rain, we head for Lumet to see if we can get a ferry to Pulua (island) Pangkor---said to be crystal clear waters for diving and snorkelling. The rain sends up lots of new smells, warm air smells, some a lot better than others!!!!!

We drive through plantations of palm, there are rows and rows of trees, you can see right through them, dead palm leaves and weeds on the floor between the trees, mile after mile,,,, no jungle here, no natural habitat left at all---sad-very sad!!!!

We arrive at Lumet, it's a passenger ferry only. Apparently there is a cargo ferry which we try to sort out, but in the end give up trying, we cannot seem to be understood. People just don't take cars on ferries or so it seems.

We book into a resort for 2 nights, it has a swimming pool. It's right on the beach but jelly fish are everywhere again. We have a swim in the pool with flashes of lightning, so back to the room. When it's time to eat we see that the hotel does vegetarian food, or so they say, but only if it contains chicken or bacon. We find good Italian restaurant, saved by the Italians yet again........

Sunday 2nd January.......swimming in pool and then to the gym, superb!

Then we go for a walk around the town, it smells (stinks) very strongly of rotting fish, everywhere is so messy with so much rubbish, it's just not pleasant to walk around.

So back to the hotel and we go swimming again, just before the monsoon rain starts. It is so heavy, after it has calmed down, we go back to our Italian place--lots of spaghetti, minestrone soup and pizza, then back to watch some Dr. Who and sleep.......

Monday 3rd.....164201........Didn't have much sleep as there was a bad storm for most of the night. Again we are travelling through miles of palm trees, standing in perfect lines, broken only by areas being logged, brown acres of soil and stripped logs. It is easy to see the devastation that is happening!! When there are a few houses we can see how high the water level is, the houses appear to be in pools..

This country is so different from the jungles of Thailand and Laos. The other thing we see is rice fields, again in straight lines, to me everywhere looks so man-made, nothing natural.

Approaching the town we see wide grass verges, with rubbish all over them. There are men strimming the grass but not picking up the rubbish, just strimming under and around it, they just don't seem to know what to do with it, or perhaps they just don't see it like me. I guess the structure is just not there, sad, in the town the storm drains are blocked with rubbish in them.

1pm......normally we avoid motorways, but as all the roads look the same, we opt for it, and yes its palm tree plantations again..

Arrival at Kuala Lumpur takes us to the Citrus hotel, in a side street off the main drag. The rooms ok and so is the price, the only problem is that you can only book by internet, how stupid, but they flatly refuse to book us in. They give us their internet code and we try to connect in the lobby, but it seems impoooible, then they tell us that if we can connect there will be a six hour wait. Not too good on customer satisfaction here, so, we give up and try next door. It's cheap, and so it should be it's horrible, dark and dirty, the cockroaches seem to like it. Well it will have to do for one night--yuk!!! I am trying hard, but this is not coming out as my favourite country!

We have all day so we go for a visit to the famous Kuala Lumpur tower for a view of the city, 276 metres, its worth it, very impressive. Included in the price is a turn on a formula one simulator, that was good fun, and also a visit to a small zoo. As usual the animals look very sad in their tiny homes, we hate most zoos, but what can you do? They have snakes and we are allowed to handle them, one the reticulated python, is so huge only Darren gets to have him around his neck, just too heavy for me and Beverley. Then we get to see a hairless Tikus Belander, I checked it out on the internet it's an enormous hamster!!!

Tuesday 4th ....164341......7.30am and we are queuing for tickets to go up the famous Petronas towers. We meet a lovely couple in the queue, and start chatting. Carol and David , they have been visiting their son in Oz, and tell us it's a wonderful place. After 3hrs we get tickets for 1.30pm. We go shopping to fill the 3 hour wait, we buy a couple of music albums. Eventually we arrive back at the towers. Then after watching an advertising film on Petronas we are allowed to go up to the bridge. The lift takes us up 41 floors in 41 seconds, it sounds amazing, but, to be honest, I didn't feel anything, Then onto the famous walkway, good view, interesting, I thought it was going to be really scary but it wasn't, bit of a disappointment really.....the best bit of the trip was meeting Carol and David.

We continue our drive south and stop at Port Dickson, checked out a few places and ended up in room which opens onto the beach, its good but I notice that the door to the beach doesn't lock, so we change room. They also have a swimming pool, we are about to go for a swim when I notice the fridge isn't working, I wait in room while Darren and Beverley go to pool, they are very efficient and have it fixed it minutes. I change and head for the pool, it closes for the evening as I arrive, so we go in the sea instead, it is so warm!!!!

Wednesday 5th ...hot..hot...swim in pool, then a walk, and back in the pool. Time to do some work as we can get on line. We start to sort out the paperwork for the Oz visas,,,,,police checks and medical forms........

Thursday 6th.... We print off the police forms and post to England. We have managed to get appointments for our medicals in K.L. on Monday. It's all a bit scary, hope they don't find anything wrong, I'm sure Beverley and Darren are ok. I'm worried I might let them down if I'm not passed as fit. Decide to stop thinking and head back to pool.

Friday 7th........164440....11.30am off to Melaka for a couple of days to check out the ferry for Sumatra. We get a puncture and stop to get it repaired, Darren notices that the price of the tyres is very good and decides to buy 4 new ones---£320---can't complain we thought that was going to be a lot pricier.

 Melaka, looks a very run down place and after trying many guest houses and hotels we opt for an expensive, Pergola Hotel, £50 a night, with-out a pool. The room is so big -- the space is great, Beverley has her bed around the corner with some long awaited privacy, and it's all wonderfully clean!!! Me and Beverly have a go at tie dying a vest--works well...out for meal, back for film.....having no joy with the internet or ferries.

Saturday 8th.......Lazy morning and then we walked to a shopping mall, here you can buy anything you want, which we did----one jar marmite---one sling shot and 3 very, very old films--(-Beetlejuice and two cartoons)===back to room and more tie dying!!!!

Sunday 9th.....164496...we left the lovely Pergola hotel at 10.30am and aim for K.L.

We arrive and spend hours looking for the hospital; eventually we find it, and also a hotel with-in walking distance. Again this place is expensive, but at least we won't have to use a taxi for the hospital, or search for a parking space for James, which in the middle of K.L. is not easy! We have a suite, which has a kitchen with a micro-wave and kettle and a sink. Bringing in our small portable gas cooker means I can cook some decent meals, this should save us a bob or two, and breakfast is included. We have plenty of space and it's very clean. There are two double beds, separated by shelving and a television. A bathroom with shower and a small sit in bath, with a pull out washing line which is another money saving device! OOOh I'm easily pleased! There is a balcony with a great view of James many floors down. Higher up is a gym and a pool on the roof, I wonder if we will have the time to use them.

Monday 10th. Walked to the hospital. We have chest x rays, blood tests, urine test, full check up examination, eye sight tests and loads of paperwork, all this is put onto the computer and sent off to be checked by the visa people, the doctor, a lovely lady, says all is well and we have passed----what a relief, it is 5pm, we walk back to hotel.......Now we can start searching for a ferry that can take James to Australia!!!!!!!

Tuesday 11th....164604.....10.30am off to Klang, it's raining a bit. The news has told us that South Thailand and North Malaysia are flooded and more rain is forecast for days ahead, here and in Indonesia. They are having the worst ever floods in Oz!!

At port Klang we can only get a container for the car if we take off the tents, so we decide to try Melaka.

The expensive hotels have made it pleasant for me and Beverley in Malaysia, otherwise everywhere is dirty and run down with bars on the windows, or so it seems to me. The back streets are the worst all concrete with hundreds of air conditioner units, so ugly, but no doubt necessary. It makes me feel unsafe. Darren on the other hand sees past all of this, nothing seems to bother him, he would quite happily live here! I miss the green fields and the beauty, and the safe feeling of Villajou.

A big storm now with thunder lightning and flash flooding on roads..........we find nice hotel (hotel Kozi) and have a great Chinese meal......

Wednesday 12th.......... 164770   I have been reading up on Indonesia, there are 11,508 uninhabited islands,,,,,6,000   with populations and 129 active volcanoes and 10 per cent of the worlds forest cover-----wow I thought there was only about a dozen islands! ,

We cannot find a car ferry at Melaka, so it's off to Singapore!!!!!

Thursday 13th January.........164902........We drive past the hotel Kozi for a third time trying to find our way to the bridge. There are signposts for Woodlands, which is the first place in Singapore but no actual signposts or mention of Singapore.

Found it! At 12.05pm we leave Malaysia----Singapore customs ask us for our Malaysian insurance, we explain how we have tried to purchase it, but have been denied. They say we cannot buy insurance for Singapore without Malay insurance first. We say ok can we buy some--- no of course not, that is too easy.

Then comes the Carnet de passage--all they have to do is stamp it to say the car has entered Singapore. We cannot believe what happens next, after spending an hour looking at it they decide to get some more official guys to look at it. They are literally looking at it, staring at the paper, as if waiting for some magical event. Now four of them are looking at it, studying it deeply. Every so often three of them go around the corner, standing behind a pillar, (I want to shout "I can see you" - I bite my tongue) they chat for a few minutes, then they come back and resume staring at it. Two hours have passed. It is difficult to sit here in front of them holding back facial impressions and comments. I find this difficult to believe, we have passed through so many borders without being able to speak the language, where the officials have not been able to read our documents or perhaps never seen a European car, or for that matter people. Here they speak and read perfect English, but choose not to communicate.

After one more hour they stamp it and we are told that we will have to enter Singapore by taxi, sort out all the papers and then return to fetch the car. They send us back to Malaysia. Nobody will stamp the car back into Malaysia, because nobody is there to do it. We see a kiosk that is open so we ask for Malaysian insurance, but no, you cannot buy it on the border, so we are forced to drive without it again. As we enter we are stopped by the police, they say we can buy insurance at garages and direct us to one, at last! Of course they want paying for this, or as they say, just something to remember us by, we say, no way, and drive off. I'm glad we did that because at the garage we are told that no garages sell insurance and they kindly give us another set of directions!!!!! These directions do not pan out, so we just keep stopping at any shop with pictures outside that looks like they sell car insurance. We pull up, Darren stays with the car and I go and ask. Eventually we find insurance £12 for one month,,,,,stage one complete!!!!!!

Friday 14th January..................164941........................We take a local taxi to the special taxi rank where they can drive us into Singapore. We are driven across the bridge and through customs, on for about half an hour to take us to the AA. Here we purchase insurance---£150 for three weeks, we produce our Malay insurance, but this is not needed--surprise surprise!! Then we have to purchase an ICP == International circulation permit == about £30.....then (our favourite) they ask for the Carnet de passage. Darren gives it to them and explains to them what they need to do. The lady who is chosen to deal with us, is very confused as to whether she has to tear off the slip at the bottom of the page first, or the one at the top of the page and them staple it all back together----duhhhh--for some reason Homer Simpson comes to mind.

We go back in the taxi. Darren had verbally agreed a figure of 80 dollars (about £40) with the driver, on arrival back in Malay, he decides to change it to 120 dollars,,,,,,needless to say, Darren was not happy-----he did not pay the extra!!!!.

Back for James, and then to pizza hut for a very late 2pm breakfast.

4.10pm, here we go again, we leave Malaysia=====entering Singapore Darren gives them the stamped and passed Carnet, Singapore insurance, Malaysian Insurance, passports, log book, custom forms, and the ICP, now they are talking about extra road tax, and they inform us that we have ten free days after which we will have to pay 10 dollars a day to be here!!!!!!!!

This is our 25th country and has got to be the worst crossing, so far! Today 7 hours plus yesterday 5 hours.

Now at 6pm it is 12 hours and these people speak English----eventually we get through. Then customs pull us in, they find 8 very small cans of beer. With all the confusion and delays, nothing was ever mentioned about what we could take into Singapore, yes it was our responsibility to find out, so we pay up, and boy did they sting us! Never mind we are in.

Now to find a hotel, this becomes difficult as the word "family" doesn't seem to have any meaning here!!!! When we say we want to share a room, the looks and the comments are unbelievable, it's not just that they want to charge us for two rooms, they really seem to think we are doing something wrong. Two beds and a blanket on the floor is the best we can do for £80........in the night Darren develops a very high temperature and is coughing, sneezing and vomiting!!!!

Saturday 15th......Darren is ill all day, me and Beverley go for bread, the hotel is next to a Durian shop and the whole area smells of rotting flesh---oh how we love Singapore-----by the evening Darren is a little better but Beverley is feeling rough......

Sunday 16th Jan......164980....Darren is still very rough but a little better, Beverley has very high temperature, they are both on tablets. We have to change hotel today as they are fully booked. We find a better, cheaper hotel with 3 single beds in a line, just like a little hospital room, and now I have joined in, and we all have a very bad case of flu...........

Mon--Tues—We manage to just drink a little water. We are a little better by the evening and check e-mails. We have to go straight back to K.L. my chest x rays are bad, and need more tests, could be TB or cancer or who knows what-scary!!!!

Wednesday 19th.....165002......11am back to Malaysia, We are made to fill the tank up before leaving Singapore, because the diesel in Malaysia is cheaper than Singapore. We leave without anyone signing the carnet out of Singapore or into Malaysia, there is no-one on the border to do it, this we know is going to cause us problems, but if there is no-one there, no-one to ask, what can you do?

Singapore is a huge city of skyscrapers and as we re-enter Malaysia the amount of sky is noticeable.

We arrive at the clinic at 4.40pm (closes at 5) I run in to get an appointment while Darren and Beverley try to park. The doctor is there, she is very surprised to see me as they have received no e-mails from Oz. I explain what we have been told and she says that the x-ray has white dots on it which looks like something occupational---like a miner, or a builder and nothing to do with TB or smoking or cancer. She phones immigration and they say they want to know how the damage was done, so I will have to see specialist........booked in for 10.30am Friday.

Thursday.20th........We have booked back into same hotel as before, do a little shopping - we leave the computer in a shop for the guy to put on all the Sims games for Beverley - we are all still very tired and not well, Beverley goes to bed exhausted.

Friday 21st........9.30am. Beverley is just waking up, she has slept for 15 hours solidly, she says she feels a bit better, she decides to stay in bed while we go to the appointment.

The specialist, Dr. Manon, tells us he took his medical exams at Heartlands hospital, Birmingham, he seems a nice chap. We explain to him that we think the damage to my lungs could of been done by the woodburner and living inside the house while rebuilding it, and building walls using traditional methods, tons of lime and sand. He agrees and says that it makes sense, but he thinks immigration will not accept an all clear with-out further tests to prove that it is not TB and there is nothing wrong with me, well if that's the way it is.

I have to go for an x-ray in a big machine so that they can see slices of my lungs. They lie me on a bed and stick a needle in the back of my hand so they can put coloured dye into me. The nurse puts my hands above my head and tells me not to move, and to follow the instructions...ok says I....what instructions? After a while with the machine moving up and down, a loud voice shouts through a microphone and says "hold your breath" oh those instructions, I nearly fell of the bed. Then they put the coloured dye into me, telling me I may go warm all over, they can say that again--hot or what!!! After that they take some more blood and ask me to spit into a plastic tub, I need to do this (spit) for the next couple of days so that they can grow cultures, which will take at least 6 weeks.

Back to hotel. Beverley is much better so we all go to collect the computer. It's all done, brilliant. Darren couldn't load the games because the drive is no good. Beverley is very happy we have also bought a game called Dracula origin, she has wanted this for ages--- since France. I don't know who is the happiest, Beverley who has all her games sorted, or Darren, who doesn't have to try and get them loaded any longer!!!!!!!!!!!!!!!!!

Saturday22nd----Sun----Mon----Tuesday---dropped phlegm at hospital and paid out about £360,,,,not much else to tell.

Wednesday 26th.....Started out to visit the famous Bird park, my idea, but Darren and Beverley won and we spent the day at Tesco......

Thursday 27th......To the Bird park, and it was really good, well I enjoyed it a lot. Beverley thought it was cool when she was covered in parrots and she had a photo taken with an owl on her shoulder, she's always loved owls. We had a nice meal and a few laughs, especially with the toucans flying in to pinch our dinner, they are so cheeky. It was good to get out for the day........

Friday 28th January 2011 .....Darren has a bad back and finding it uncomfortable to sit, no doubt one of the penalties for living in a car!

Saturday 29th.......Got the car welded again, hopefully fixed this time. The guys actually did as Darren asked.

Sunday 30th ....Shopped at Carrefour, just like being back in France when we used to visit Limoges to go to Carrefour, bought some more Simpsons videos. It's been raining all day, a bit miserable really.

We have heard that you can volunteer to work with the orang-utans at Sepilok in Borneo, where we intend to visit. Such an exciting idea that I sent an email to them to check it out. They said yes, but, wanted us to pay £3000 each for the privilege!! I guess so many people want to do it they can afford to charge, but what a disappointment!

Monday 31st........165313..........Colin and Chrissy have put us in touch----by email---to a man in Klang, he is shipping them to Brisbane, also he has lots of Landy parts, so today we go to see him. His name is Assir and his nick name is 'one dollar' he is an extremely interesting person, and also seems a kind man. He has visited over 80 countries on his travels, a few more than us! He owns a BMW bike and a 4wd Toyota. There is plenty of chatting over a cup of tea. Then we follow his brother Abul, another nice chap, to a Land Rover scrap yard. This place is half way between KL and Klang. Here we meet some more really helpful people. We now have our shipping agent and the place to strip down, clean and prepare James for Oz....brilliant.

Now all we need is the visa!!!!!

While chatting with Assir, we told him about us driving into Singapore, he said it was unheard of, the only way in is to put your car on a trailer to be taken to the port. He told us the tents on the roof would never be allowed in, well they hadn't asked us about the tents so we had said nothing!!!! Apparently no motor that has a sleeping facility is ever allowed in, and no motors with anything that has ever been modified. We called our James more of a personalized, adapted version, rather than a modification. How did we ever get in to Singapore, we will never know.

On return to KL we receive an email to say that Beverley's x-ray had still not been sent. We walk back to the hospital for an answer, they say that Australian immigration are holding things up because they will not accept the x-ray without a reference number but will not issue one. Also they will not answer as to whether the hospital should send it electronically or by post,....there is nothing we can do.

We have bought a mobile phone so we can leave a number with the hospital, should they need us for anything, and have booked ourselves a 2 week break in Sabah, at Sandakan, we are going to see the orangutans........

Tuesday 1st February....Public holiday for Malaysia today, nothing to report.

Wednesday 2nd.....Chinese new year.... Beverley bought a beautiful white dress and a black jacket, new shoes and a necklace.....I bought sandals and a necklace. We had to fill a few hours while Darren had a new tribal tattoo on his arm and an old tattoo redone. They look fabulous, he is very pleased, with the tattoos that is!

Thursday 3rd Feb......Saw some Chinese celebrations, a huge dancing lion and very loud drums, in fact so loud it spoilt it, it was just uncomfortable to stand and watch. Beverley bought a hat....

Friday 4th Feb.....Drove to F.R.I.M. ---Forestry Research Institute of Malaysia. It took us ages to find it, we had gone to do the canopy walk but it was closed until March. So we did a forest walk instead and we saw some massive ants, at least an inch and a half long. Beverley got the creeps with the ants and then she saw leeches---luckily for Beverley it was only a short walk. She was extremely pleased to be back in our room. We watched some more "ello ello"....funny!

Saturday 5th Feb. More shopping!!!! We took the wii machine to have it modified so that we can play the cheap copy games.......

Sunday 6th Feb......Bored---bored !!!!! Started packing--bored!!!

Monday 7th....Same.....picked up wii and some new games......

Tuesday 8th... Shopping----packing----got e-mail to say Beverleys' x-ray still not sent.....went back to hospital to get the same story, still nothing we can do........

Wednesday 9th Feb.....up at 4am for flight at 7.30am.

It was a good flight, we arrive in Sandakan at 10.30am---looks like what I think of as typical Malaysia, there are adverts everywhere for "Nippon Paint" but I cannot see any evidence of anyone using any paint anywhere!!! We find a nice hotel with a big room and a restaurant on the roof, we all eat well, we are all very tired and irritable so we go back to our room, shower, then watch a film on the tv and sleep......

Thursday 10th February........Caught the bus to Sepilok jungle resort. We had seen all the advertising, and read up on the place. Me and Beverley were excited and looking forward to a couple of days of luxury. In reality our room was very tiny, consisting of a single bed and a bunk bed---a light and a fan and a window. All the walls decorated with little white cobwebs. The toilets and showers were only two minutes away---it was all just about ok, but what a disappointment!!! (We later discovered that there was other accommodation that would have been preferable, but we had not been offered this, probably as we are backpackers!!!!)

We slept and awoke to find ourselves surrounded by jungle, all looked better after a sleep. As in the brochure, it was only a five minute walk to the orang-utan rehabilitation centre. Walking along we saw monkeys playing in the trees, it's brilliant to see wild animals having fun. The centre was closed for an hour, so we bought an ice cream and sat and watched the trees, and were lucky enough to see orangutans , a mother and baby in one tree and a young juvenile in another, who climbed about watching us, considering our every move, scrutinizing us with his beautiful brown eyes.

After a while we decided to walk up the road to the forestry reserve --on the way, running up the trees and along the power line, we saw a very handsome black squirrel with a red underbelly, stunning. At the reserve there was a canopy walk which took us up and through the tree tops. It was breathtaking. I have always wanted to go up into the tree tops since I saw David Attenborough do it!!!! After which we walked through orchid gardens. I saw the vanilla orchid with vanilla pods, what a great way to discover where vanilla comes from. Making a cake will never be the same again. There were plenty of other things to see, including some lovely green lizards running and hiding.

 The time quickly came to return to the resort for food. Nothing we ordered for Beverley turned up, and the staff were not in the slightest bit interested, so we all just shared what had arrived. We finished with biscuits in our room. Shame the location of the restaurant was stunning........

Friday 11th Feb.....To the orangutan reserve, firstly we watched a video about the place, after which we went along a boardwalk to the feeding stations in the trees. Spotted one orangutan waiting and watching. A man arrived with bananas and sugar cane, he climbed up the steps to the boards around the tree and sat quietly. We watch. There are ropes attached to the trees going into the forest, one of the ropes started to sway, we were very fortunate as five orangs of different sizes and colours arrive, it was a fabulous sight to see, we took heaps of really great photos. We stayed for quite a while. I asked myself if this was real, us in Borneo with orangutans, I feel so privileged.

Back on bus to Sandakan to catch the 1 o'clock bus to Sukau to a jungle retreat.....by 4,30pm it still had not arrived so we gave up. We had been talking to a German backpacker called Thomas, we decided to travel together tomorrow........

Saturday 12th.. This time the mini bus arrives on time-12pm- and we arrive at the retreat at 2.30pm, starving. We discover that dinner is at 7pm and there are no shops. I have a bag with biscuits and a loaf of bread and a pot of jam, so many times have these basic foods come in and saved us. The room is pretty much the same as Sepilok. Darren goes on the river trip to see the proboscis monkey. I thought about going with him. It was raining, the sloping bank to the boat was very slippery, the others were laughing as they slid down the bank and jumped into the boat. I suddenly felt weak and tired, I did not want, or have the energy, to rush down to the boat, Beverley wasn't keen either.

So that was decided, we stayed behind and read our books and stared into the trees, we saw animals, insects by the ton, birds, including some huge rhinoceros hornbills. We drank tea and really enjoyed ourselves whilst staying dry!

Sunday 13th.....8.30am off to catch bus to Semporna. We arrive at the pier, there are many dive shops. We ask about the different dives, it seems very expensive and it doesn't have a very friendly atmosphere here. Next we try the Dragon Hotel, as usual we ask to see the room, but they refuse saying its hotel policy that we pay first. I wonder why, it's unusual, what have they got to hide? I ask again, but they will not budge, we leave. Then we walk up into the town to find a shop called Scuba Junkie, they are very helpful and happy and we soon get booked in for dives, and find a hotel. It is completely different, great!

Monday 14th.....8am and we are on a fast boat to an Island called Mabul, fantastic, exciting, beautiful. Darron does three dives, and loves it. He sees masses of fish plus five turtles. Me and Beverley snorkel, but without the snorkel, we use only masks and have named it "goggling"---we love it,, the warm clear sea, the coral and so many different types of fish it is magical----what a brilliant day.

Unfortunately I didn't listen to Beverley, and ignored her advice on buying new sun cream, we got burnt!!!!

Tuesday 15th.....Rest day, booked more dives for tomorrow....

Wednesday 16th......8am and we are on another fast boat, this time to Sibuan Island.

An almost unbelievable place - a perfect desert island. It's an incredible sight, about 4oo metres long and 5o metres wide, at the widest point. A picturebook scene, easy to imagine Johny Depp strolling along. There are five huts belonging to sea gypsies from the Philippines. Swaying in the warm breeze, coconut trees--which the children will climb to get you a fresh coconut. This produces a little income for them, they also clean the barnacles off the bottom of the boats. Whilst Darren is diving, we walk around the island, on the hot white sand, it's so small! We are in and out of the turquoise warm water, goggling. There is so much life, we find the clown fish we wanted to see in the coral (from the film Nemo). Scores of brightly coloured fish, of all shapes and sizes, are swimming around us. Some come right up to our masks, to have a look. Others touch us and try a taste, just a little suck, no teeth. There are so many star fish lying on the sea floor it is almost a carpet effect. We see parrot fish, ghost fish, yellow snappers, and so many others. Goodness knows what Darren is seeing on the dive. This is one of the worlds finest diving areas, and it's easy to see why.

What a perfect day!!!

Thursday 17th ....Up at 5am to catch bus to Kota Kinabula---the capital city of Sabah---known as KK---not really looking forward to going back to a city, where's that beach gone? Wondering what the roads are going to be like, we have had a terrific storm for the last few hours and this is an eight hour trip.

Nine and a half hours later we arrive, the bus had brake problems coming down the mountain, so we had to stop a couple of times. I actually quite enjoyed the bus ride, I love watching out the window, never get bored. We try a couple of cheap hotels, but they are really disgusting!!!! We jump in taxi to centre of town, this cheap hotel is O.K. we order a pizza in, and sort ourselves out. Later we go for a walk and find two pizza restaurants and lots of diving shops. Unfortunately we have a bad night sleep due to a smelly air con!!!!

Friday 18th.....We have found a backpackers place to stay and it's clean. We have a lot more room, two double beds--tv--en-suite shower and toilet. There is a tv room with a small kitchen to make toast and coffee, plus very cheap laundry---(nice break from handwashing). Also other travellers to chat with--and it's cheaper!!!!! This is really good. We have booked diving and goggling for tomorrow.........

Saturday 19th......We take a 15 minute fast boat to Sapi island, it is gorgeous....(not as good as Semporna, but nothing is). Darren does 2 dives while we goggle. Me and Beverley take a break for a cup of tea. We see five huge monitor lizards, they look quite scary with their forked tongues, also a few macaque monkeys are scrounging about. Darren returns and we jump back on the boat to go to a different island for lunch. Darren goes off for another dive and we go to goggle. The weather is changing now and we cannot see so many fish, so we go and root in hammocks and read our books while waiting for the boat-- thinking what a hard life –haha. It starts to rain and cools down a bit, but still ok. We spot two hermit crabs and we stop reading to watch them, we think they are trying to mate---who knows , but it makes good entertainment. Time comes to get back on the boat, feeling happy that it's only a short trip back to the mainland, there is a storm coming, and I don't want to be on the sea when it arrives. Evening time and we eat in the "Little Italy" restaurant. The food is excellent and so is the company. We have met up with the three backpackers we met in Semporna, Jose, Deamy, and Saskia....

Sunday 20th.....6am and we awake to the street market right outside our window. People singing and bands playing, it all sounds cheerful. By 7am we are walking around it, we see lots of animals for sale, fish, turtles, hamsters, rabbits, chicks, kittens but the saddest of all is all the puppies. Some in cages, some in cardboard boxes--if only we could buy them all --- good job we can't!!!!

We go to get some cash but several ATM's refuse us, so we phone the bank. It was our own fault, we had agreed with the bank to keep the ATM working for three months in Asia and the date has expired. That passed so quickly, after a few security questions all is ok and the ATM works for us.

Darren goes to have a tattoo of a dragon done on his leg, meanwhile me and Beverley go shopping. Beverley finds some really pretty paper butterflies to go on her hat. I think this hat is going to become quite a creation.

Monday 21st----Up and out early to catch the 8am bus back to Sandakan, it takes us 7 hours.....

Tuesday 22nd.....We walk around the town and visit the museum. There is a new section being opened, so they have dancers and people in traditional dress sitting in the longhouses weaving mats. Then we go to tourist info, just trying to fill the day. In the evening we have take away curry and rice with rotis,, this is from a local Malay cafe-the best and cheapest way to eat, for £4 we have enough for 4 people plus drinks, can't complain.

Wednesday 23rd.....Caught the bus to the crocodile farm, we weren't expecting much but it was horrible. On the way in they asked us to pay far too much, we refused, then they tried to charge Beverley as an adult, although the sign clearly stated that children are 12 and under. After another few words we were in. All the animals are in small, dirty pens, with food hanging just out of their reach, which of course you had to pay for. The question is - are we helping these animals by paying money or just prolonging their suffering? The living conditions were appalling--there were two otters jumping and screaming for food, the fish were hung in jars so that they could see them. We emptied all the jars into their tiny pool and watched them diving in and out catching and eating them, sheer happiness, for a few minutes. We were being followed around by a man in dark sun-glasses, he was watching our every move, and checking we paid for the food. After a while this became very uncomfortable. Darren asked him to go away and leave us alone, he obviously didn't want to, but Darren convinced him otherwise. After that we left. Then back to the Malay cafe for our take away, we ate it in our room watching the discovery channel on tv......

Thursday 24th.....We catch our 10.25am flight back to K.L. and taxi back to the Peninsular apartments, good old James the Landy is sitting outside awaiting our return. It's lovely to be back where I cannot smell the drains venting outside there are no smells of moth balls in the rooms---I really hate that. The bathroom and toilet are clean and not shouting for a bottle of cream cleanser!!!!! The hotel offers us a cheaper rate if we stop for more than two weeks----which we are not----last time we stayed for a month and asked for a better rate but they refused, how annoying. We settle in and then taxi over to Times Square to buy a couple of small remote control helicopters to play with and have a pizza.......

We all have a bad night sleep as the people in the next room were having a party!!!!!

Friday 25th.....We tell reception about the party in the night, they say the people are leaving........we taxi back to town and renew our car insurance, and get one of the helicopters fixed........Back to the hotel and we are told that the party people are going to stop another night and continue their party, we are advised to move room. We don't want to do this as we have so much stuff in the room, and why should we it's not us causing the problem. We are told that the party people are Malaysians and we are not, so we have to move, or put up with it. We ask for a reduction for the inconvenience of moving but they refuse, so we move, this is now our last night here---shame but not a lot we can do about it!!!!

Saturday 26th Feb.....Up at 7am and on the road for 11am.......165498....James is behaving well, no problems. We are heading for the Cameron Highalnds---up the mountains in the jungle. After about 100 miles of normal road we turn off and start climbing up a steep very windy road, this continues for a good hour and we are well into sticky, hot jungle, it's like being back in Laos---we love it. We keep going, it cools down but still very pleasant. We come to a small-town called Ringlet ,and on driving through, we count over 20 Land Rovers, they are everywhere, James fits in very well........

Sunday 27th February.......Yesterday evening we arrived in Tana Rata and found a guest house called Twin Pines....very cheap and very clean with a beautiful garden to sit in, full of flowers. Today we have a lazy morning, it is cooler here just right for Tshirts. We drive to Ringlet to see some more Land Rovers and we find a little museum called The Time Tunnel. Here we find out about the history behind Land Rovers. There are approximately 5000 in this area, but we don't know why? Then we go to the Smokehouse Hotel for a cup of tea (£7 for 3 cups!!) Chrissy and Colin had told us about it, and had said how English it was, and they were right, it's like being in the Cotswolds, the hotel is mock Tudor---so so English....

Monday 28th....Darren fixed the car--power steering pump---then we drove again to Ringlet and bought a steering damper. Onto the butterfly and insect park, then the bee farm where I bought honey for Darren (me and Beverley can't stand it). Next we picked strawberries at one of the many strawberry farms, which I and Beverley love, but not Darren . To finish the day we have more Indian food, which we all love, followed by a film and bed......

Tuesday 1st March......More strawberry picking and eating! Afterwards we visited a huge tea plantation, rows and rows of bushes, covering acres, a stunning sight. Then we walked around the factory learning how the tea is processed, and then, of course, had a cup of tea and a slice of cake!!!!

Wednesday 2nd March.....165720.....11am and we are off to the Taman Negara (national park), we expect it to take us about 5 hours in James. The jungle park is said to be exactly the same as it was 130 million years ago and just as the dinosaurs saw it. As we leave Tana Rata we pass through Ringlet , there is no jungle here but many miles of white polytunnels and acres of palm plantations.

12pm and it starts to get jungly , then we find ourselves passing two huge logging trucks. We arrive at Kuala Tahan, a small town by the river. Across the river, which is only about 3ft deep, is Taman Negara and the Taman Negara jungle resort. We decide to check it out and take a look so we jump into one of the many small boats, 20p each to cross. We climb the stone steps, there is a welcoming party, but not for us, just for the paying tourists who choose to arrive at the same time as us. I enter the crowded reception and ask if there are any rooms available, I am told I will have to wait until all the paying guests are sorted first. Well that's when they lost my vote, I pick up a leaflet on the way out the resort, it costs about £350 a night, not quite what we are looking for anyway! Next to the park rangers office, we find that they only charge 20p each to enter the park, that sounds more like it. We go back across the river to find a room, we will visit the park tomorrow. After trying a few places we find the Dorian chalet park. It has everything and is clean, with a little restuarant, all for £10 a night!!! That's quite a saving!

Thursday 3rd March....Beverley is not looking forward to today as she is worried about the insects and leeches, but not too bothered about the tigers, leopards, wild boar, elephants and rhino. I guess she's right though, as there is not much chance of seeing the big animals, whereas the insects are guaranteed. I say it cannot be that bad as many people go on the walks every day, I hope I am right!

We drive to the river, cross on the boat, and start the walk. It begins with a wooden walkway, after about 1km we reach the canopy walkway. It's in several sections, made up of a plank about 18 inches wide with rope and mesh on the sides, 400 metres long and 25 to 40 metres high. It is fantastic and scary, but what a privilege to be able to do this, the views I cannot describe (see google images) .

Friday 4th March....Lazy morning then back across river and into jungle for a swim and a paddle in the river. Beverley has caught a head cold, and she is not feeling too brilliant!!..

Drove down to town to book a night safari, sounds quite exciting. On the way, on a narrow track road Darren reverses to allow a car to pass. On going forward he clips the post on the front of a wooden house, it is holding up the roof, doesn't look too bad ,not much damage, I hope. As it is getting dark, Darren promises to go back in the morning and put it right.

On the night safari Darren, along with some others, sits on the roof of the car. Me and Beverley opt for the inside where we can hang out of the windows, without falling off, or getting wet in the rain. The way is lit by a guy on the roof with a big torch, he knows where to look. We see four leopard cats, think it' a pretty rare skillit cat. One with a kitten, the car scared the mother cat away and the kitten seemed to want to get into the car, it kept approaching us and crying.

We are driven around the vast palm plantation. The huge leaves on some of the trees have fallen down around the bark of the trees making them look like skirts and with the lightening in the background they look, to me, like gigantic aliens. We see several cows and another leopard cat, then back out onto the road again. In the trees at the side of the road, the man shines his light, I see something moving. There right in front of us, so close, are two black panther cats, wow! We also saw an owl and by the side of the road a normal cat carrying a tiny kitten, but I am still smiling at seeing panthers in the wild, really did not think we would be so lucky to see those magnificent animals!!!!!

Saturday 5th March.......165883 - Darren goes to check how much damage he did last night, they were very happy with £80, that should cover it all.

 We pack up and drive through Maran, to the east coast. We pass through the plantations on one of the twistiest roads we've been on. We stop for a cup of tea, but forget to say black and no sugar, it arrives with a thick layer of condensed milk in the bottom of the glass and I can't guess how many sugars, just a sip was enough for us!! They do seem to love the sugar here.

After Maran near the town of Kuantan we find a "Giant" supermarket and stop to re-fill the fridge, and we found a pizza hut. Stuck in traffic we look at the mileage, we've driven 26,680 miles and the circumference of the earth is about 25,000 milles. Looking at the spelling on signs we see a klinik and a pol i tek nik, a koleg, a stesen (station) a lori and a bas (bus) --love it!!!!

We arrive at the sea-side and find a lovely big room with a very large balcony. The place is alive with a market and stalls, in front of the sea. There are artists drawing and people singing. We go for a swim, the beach is clean and the sea is almost the temperature of bath water!! Excellent --.

Sunday 6th March...up at 9.30am it is so hot!! Too hot to go out, we put on a film and eat toast. This is no good we have to go out, we go for a walk on a boardwalk to a second cove and have a swim. We notice that the cliff at the side of the wooden boardwalk is on fire and we don't want to get trapped, can't see any other way off the beach, so we decide to return. Nobody seems to be worried about the fire, although there are loads of people looking at it.

We take another swim in the very warm sea and play in the surf . Later we go and eat Indian food for dinner, still wearing our wet shorts and T.shirts. Back to the room, to read books on the balcony, but it is just too hot, we have cold showers, if you can call them that as the water is tepid. Then watch some more tv., now what can we do? After a while we go for a drive, about 40-50km up the coast to a place called Cherating. Here there is another lovely beach, will probably move there tomorrow.......looks like a big storm on the way........

Monday 7th March....166061...up and out by 11am to Cherating where we find a great chalet, and a reggae bar that sells pizza and pasta, brilliant. We take another warm swim and a fish foot massage in a small lagoon, the tiny fish tickling our toes, nibbling at our feet, oh its lovely! Beverley is better, but now Darren has a runny nose.......

Tuesday 8th March...Two swims today, me and Beverley wore our goggles so we could dive into the waves and sit and watch the waves come over us, it's great fun. Lunch time, we go for lunch at a cafe on the beach called "Don't tell Mama" it served great food. The only thing that isn't perfect is the mosquitoes, it rained this morning so out they come, we are covered in bites - again!!

Wednesday 9th March....166093...Time for us to move on and take James to the garage ----(we sent an e-mail to the doctor on Monday as we are waiting for the final medical results, no answer as yet)....James needs a few repairs and a good clean before he can be shipped to Australia. He will need to be stripped and scrubbed, poor thing.

The rain is really heavy, it is coming through the back doors, there is about one inch of water on top of the carpet!!! We are all still itching from our mosey bites, Beverley has a quick count up and finds 48--no--49--no -54 on her arms and legs, we ask her to stop counting!!!!!

We arrive at the garage "Black Hawk" there are more Land Rovers here than---well I don't know!!! This is the Malaysian Land Rover club. It is run by Alyna and Artek, they are very friendly and say we can stay here for free. We move into the office, there are two settees and several desks, they have camp beds we can use, we have internet. Outside, just a minute away are toilets and a shower, they make us so welcome - even cook us a meal,, so so kind.....

Thursday 10th....we phone the doctor for our results at 9am, ask us to ring again at 10.30 then ask us to ring again at 2.30 then ask us to ring back Monday. To say the least it is frustrating!!!!

We keep cleaning and preparing for the trip, this is what we do, but are we going to get the visas, is the trip to Australia on, or will we have to go somewhere else, who knows?

Friday 11th...It is raining and we are very bored. We see on the BBC news about the earthquake and tsunami in Japan, those poor people Have got to say I'm glad we are not in Oabah anymore, but we are still under tsunami warning!!!   Bored, bored bored!!!

Saturday 12th....Darren has been working on cleaning the car in between the storms and me and Beverley are managing to find a few things to do, but by the evening we are all bored, again. It seems the less we do the less we can be bothered to do, still it's not long till Monday and hopefully we should have some answers and then be able to make some plans..........

Sunday 13th March......Another day at the garage... James is now completely empty, even the seats are out. Darren has cleaned, scrubbed, filled with filler and painted, the wheels have been off and cleaned behind, panels taken off and chairs cleaned. All of our belongings---apart from what's in the office---are on a tarpaulin on the floor. We have boxes and bags and dozens of plastic carrier bags, the bags are tied at the top so almost impossible to open without ripping them. We are going to buy some new, solid, boxes and repack everything. Until those boxes arrive there is nothing I can do except try to keep it all dry, it has taken us a year to collect all these bits and pieces, they mean a lot to us, but at the moment it's just a mess.

At this point, a reporter, a very friendly Chinese man, arrives, he takes photo after photo of James, and us, and our mess, to put in his newspaper. Before I've had time to tidy anything, a very friendly lady reporter arrives, she does the same. We will probably never see the outcome anyway. We've been told before, that we've been in Land Rover monthly and have never seen that!!!!

Thunder is rolling again and black clouds arriving......every day it's hot in the morning and rain in the afternoon.

Another night of not sleeping too well. I have moved from the camp bed to the settee, this is more comfortable, and I have trained myself to ignore the ants, who share my nest. Most nights I have another regular visitor, a browny, orange jungle squirrel, he/she runs around the room checking to see if we have left any food out. The first time we met I was lying on my back, awake listening to the tap, tap, tap of tiny feet. He pounced onto my chest and stared into my face and I stared into his. He weighed practically nothing, he sat there for what seemed a full minute, then he took a vertical take off, and was gone. It was wonderful; from then on I have listened for him.

Monday 14th. Time to see the specialist again, I telephone and have an appointment for tomorrow.

More thunderstorms.

Tuesday 15th.......We borrow a car to get us into Kuala Lumpur. Doctor Manon says that all the tests have come back negative and I am fit, he will get the report typed up and we can collect it tomorrow, what a relief for us all!!!!

Wednesday 16th March.... Back to the hospital to collect the report and take to other hospital to pass it on to the panel doctor Dr. Surrinder. She reads the report and says that is the end, there is nothing more that they can do, except to pass the report on. Well that's all we can do..

It has taken three years to complete all the paperwork for our visas, now all we can do is wait for a yes or no. Australia or England or perhaps somewhere else? Fingers crossed, I really do want to try Australia. I love Malaysia and Laos and China and Thailand, but I want to get Beverley to experience Australia, I believe it is the best country for us all. Life is one big exciting adventure, but it's time for her to settle, get some friends around her, and spend time with others, not just us!!

Thursday...more thunderstorms....

Friday 18th March..... We got the new storage boxes today, just in time everything is starting to get wet and damp with the continuous rain, have been looking forward to this, sorting out all the clothes, books and bits we have bought from all those countries.........more thunderstorms....

Saturday....I had a dream we got an e-mail, but nothing!!

Sunday 20th.... Apparently it never rains here in March,,,,,so why won't it stop?

Monday 21st March. We get an e-mail from Chistina - our agent. There seems to be a mix up with the medical tests===DIAC,,the visa people==are asking for the same tests again plus another chest x ray. I feel like crying, but don't!!! We send e-mails to try and sort it out, will have to wait and see!!!!

I see Darren going out in the car with Artek and ask if we can come, they are on their way to the local restaurant, yes we can go with them. Feels good to get out!

I have been concerned for days about Darren not eating properly, he has refused anything cooked and just had toast or a sandwich. Now I know why, they have been going out for restaurant meals every day!!!! Well no need to be concerned then!!*****************!!

Tuesday 22nd March----It's raining and we are waiting ....

Wednesday 23rd.... Saw Doctor Surrinder again today, to check what is happening. She says there is nothing else they can do. To prove it, she takes me over to the computer and explains that when the case is finished it is wiped from her screen. She calls up my name and, yes there I am, still there. She sends the information with a tap of her finger, now we wait again. Yes that's it, I have now been erased from her computer. Let's hope that is it!!!! Thankfully I went to see her today, or this could of gone on for weeks....

We had a very pleasant evening, we went to the Malaysian Land Rover AGM. We met many interesting people, and of course , the food was wonderful.

Thursday 24th ....Trying not to go any further insane, me and Beverley watched some 'Frazier' episodes, funny!!!

Friday 25th March.......We got an e-mail from Christina, our agent. Yes, yes, yes, we have visas!!!!!!!!!!!!!!! Went and bought some beer to celebrate, can't believe it—at last.

Saturday 26th th March 2011 to 31st,,,,,working on car...............................

Friday 1st April 2011.   One year ago today we left the U.K. Sometimes it feels like a few weeks, and other times, as if we have always been on the road. I miss my family and friends so much, but I also have so much to tell them about. Time to stop thinking too much!!

 Cleaned the inside of James, washed the roof lining, it was a stripy black, off white, and red from all the mosies we have managed to kill. It cleaned up quite easily, then I cleaned and sprayed the dashboard and the interior of the doors. What a facelift, and with all the work Darren has done, and the new windscreen and sidesteps, he looks 10 years younger!!!

 Tomorrow we have been invited to a Muslim wedding, in the morning. and then into the jungle for a night of camping.......

Saturday 2nd.....Not a good night, I had to get up several times with a bad stomach, and rush across the yard to the pit toiloto, great. With shaky logo and dizzliness, oh what would I give for a shiny white flush toilet!! In-between that, the tap dancing squirrel is back for his visit, well that's what it sounds like when he is scurrying around on the lino floor.

Then he would dive onto a table followed by a huge sky dive back to repeat the tap dancing, really quite entertaining. I took a couple of tablets to ensure no toilet calls today, I hope!!!!

The plan is to leave for the wedding at 10am, but this is Malaysian time-

----

We borrowed a car (from Malaysian Darren) and started out for an hours drive at 1.30pm. Artek came with us and Alyna is in with the others. We pass the Grand Prix track and manage to see some of the actual track, it is part of a huge sports complex which is still being built. Artek and Alyna have applied for 25 acres for an off roading site, negotiations still going on.

We arrive for the wedding celebrations, and we are made very welcome. There is a huge marquee in the garden of a large house, all the usual wedding trimmings. We are all sat at a table, where we are fed and given wedding cake. We take photos outside and then are invited into the house to photo the bride and groom, they make us stand with them for a photo, even though they have no idea who we are!!!.

About 3.30pm we leave to return to the garage to pick up our things for camping. On the drive back Artek is explaining to us how Malaysia works as a Muslim country. What it is to be Muslim and live here (he is not a Muslim) and what it's like for all other groups, it's fascinating, we have learnt so much.

After a long drive it is getting dark and we are nearing the campsite, we are in thick jungle travelling along muddy tracks, through rivers, up the steepest of hills, having to be winched up, and then trying to descend slowly. There are four cars (not James---he is resting, sparkling clean back at the garage) --- Darren and Beverley are loving it, and so am I. Being with other people, and in a Landy that is not your home, makes it so much more fun, all the worry is gone!!! We eventually camp by the river, a couple of huge tarpaulins are tied up to the trees and the camp beds placed underneath, we cook loads of food and have a bbq and bonfire, lots of chat and then bed—outside. What a wonderful evening.

Sunday 3rd. We all slept really well and enjoyed being outside, then washing and cleaning teeth and swimming in the river, fantastic, this is the life! Packing up after breakfast. Malaysians, it seems, eat loads of food every couple of hours. Everyone joins in and it's soon done.

The track out the jungle has been used many times by Artek and Alyna for their off road trips as the Malaysian Land Rover group, and the mud is feet thick. It takes us ages to get us all through, with winches around trees and each others cars, it really was great fun. Unfortunately Arteks' car decides to break down, but even more fun because we had to tow it out of the jungle. At one point, we stop in the mud, I look out the window to see a beautiful black orchid, what a photo. We stop at another river to clean the cars off, and eat, and swim and paddle, and then out the jungle to a garage to wait for the tow truck. The garage was next to restaurant, so another meal was ordered (not for us, we know we can't keep up with them). It has been an incredible weekend and it had been put together almost immediately when Alyna and Artek heard that we were going to be leaving on Monday 11th - and they would be in Bangkok for our last weekend, as if they hadn't already done enough for us!!!!!!!!

Monday 4th.....Tues, Wednesday 6th....confirmed the dropping off date for James and booked our flights from K.L. to Sumatra on the morning of the 12th. We are going back packing through Indonesia while James is on his sea voyage. We will work out our Australia dates after we have seen 'one dollar' in Klang (to pass on James).......

To Klang--here we go!!!!! 1.30pm we meet 'one dollar' and take James to the container. With his new coat of paint, inside and out, James is sparkling clean, uncontaminated and pristine Darron has fitted new sideotops, roof rack, and a new windscreen. It is good to see out of the front window without all the cracks, should improve the photos. We shall miss him, he has been brilliant, and of course, our home for a year.

What a car, there is no sign of all the struggles he's been through. Darren drives him into the container, a perfect fit. This is quite a relief as our car insurance and Darren's International driving licence are both out of date! "One dollar" kindly drives us back to the garage.

8.30pm. We take our friends at the garage out for a meal to say thanks. Such a bunch of people, they just accepted us into their lives, and helped us in every way they could, I'm stuck for words!!

Tuesday 12th April. Woken early by a squirrel trying to open a packet of biscuits....6am up---taxi arrives on time at 7am. I am just about to leave the office, (our home) when a massive bat swoops in through the door, it's zig zagging around the room. Now what do I do? I can't really concentrate, I think we have everything, so I prop the door open and walk towards the waiting taxi. Having time to think I realize that I have left Darren's hat, no great problem, but also a bag of rubbish for the bin. Sorry guys, not the nicest way to leave things.

It's only a one hour flight to Sumatra, and we have to collect the visa on arrival. We are asked to leave the queue and taken to an office where our fingerprints are taken. That's different, we have never been fingerprinted before, what do they think we might do? Well, we're not going to do anything wrong, so what does it matter, we are in.

Next we get some cash and become millionaires again. One bottle of water costs 8000 Indonesian rupiah. We get a taxi to the bus station, to find we have just missed the local bus, so we have to wait for a mini bus. Bit of a disappointment because we wanted to travel with the locals on the bus, quite different from a mini-bus, can't be helped.

At 12pm we pay £6 each for a five hour drive (cheap enough). The driver drives with his hand on the horn and is crazy, as they all seem to be. At 12.40pm we stop to change car which seems to take forever, the driver is having tea with his friends. At 1,10pm we are off at breakneck speed, then after a couple of minutes he slows right down and starts chatting on his phone, then back to high speed, then another stop to say hello to someone---this is going to be a long journey! Darren and

Beverley fall asleep,,,,,,,,8pm we are dropped off at a very expensive looking hotel-----clean sheets -- hot water-- pleasant restaurant, this is going to cost, but it is too late to find anywhere else. What a shame!!!

Wed 13th April.   8am breakfast, hot shower, ooh luxury.

We start walking to the bus station. A car stops and the local police sargeant - called Raymond offers us a lift. He takes us to ATM and then to mini bus-car, again not the local bus that we were going to use, maybe next time, this should be a lot more comfortable. Raymond gives us his address and phone number in case we have any problems. He tells us to pass it on to anyone we know, or hear of, that might visit his town. Again a total stranger looking out for us and other travellers, he drove miles to sort us out, how kind.

11am and we are off in a very hot car. The sun is on my arm, so I get the wet washing out and drape it over me. The smells here keep changing from diesel to sulphur to durian fruit.

We arrive at the airport to find there are no internal flights. Darren wants to take the bus, but it's at least a 35 hour trip. We are informed that the coach has a toilet, so the stops are limited. In my mind I can already smell it, and the thought turns my stomach. I know this is my weakness, but I can't do anything to stop it. Darren has no sense of smell at all, he cannot understand how it is for me, I would love to lose my sense of smell. One thing he does know is that life may be easier for all of us, if we fly.

 We book for Jakarta with Lion Air, It costs us 3 hundred pounds for the three of us. 3.30pm in the air, good flight, except for the baby next to me with a full nappy, one of lifes little jokes!

Thursday 14th April   Darren goes and checks out the trains. There is the 9.45am train tomorrow to Cirebon, on the Cirebonekspres. We spend the day walking, shopping and eating chicken on a stick.

Friday 15th April..... We arc leaving Jakarta on a 3 hour trip. This is very different from being on the road. I can see right into peoples houses, perhaps I shouldn't, but I can't resist seeing how people live. These are what we would call slums, with vast piles of rubbish everywhere. People are searching through the piles, for what I don't know.

The ticket inspector arrives, he is accompanied with a serious looking, uniformed, armed guard.

We see miles and miles of rice fields, and enormous areas of flooding. We pass a house where I see a lady with her baby in her arms. She is standing with water up to her knees, a very sad and moving sight.

We arrive and find a hotel right by the station. We try to book the train tickets for tomorrow but we are told " no trains tomorrow they all have trouble". After a walk round the shops we try again, the trains are all better now, so we book for Semabrang.

Further walking, to fill in the time, we watch a lot of police rushing about, many cars with flashing lights. We think it must be someone very important arriving at the police station. Back at the hotel we see something on the news but cannot understand the language. It's the police that we saw earlier, but it looks like something nasty has happened. We ask at reception, they explain to us that there was a suicide bomber in the police station. We must have been watching just after the explosion. It scares me to think how close we must of been , we could easily have been hurt, or perhaps noticed as foreigners, we're not anywhere near a tourist route. We decide to stay in the room, and spend the next few hours watching cartoons in Indonesian --Sponge Bob Square pants!!!!

A passing thought , James is probably on his way to Oz now.........

Sunday 17th April ...On the train and off by 8.30am. We arrive at Surabaya at 1pm. Straight away we book the tickets for South Bali, to the town of Denpasar. It's a 12 hour trip - at least- costs us 14 pounds each and leaves at 10.30pm. Nine and a half hours to fill, it's bit of a wait!!! After looking outside of the station, and not finding anything, we resign ourselves to the station seats. Me and Beverley spot two massage chairs, and decide to have a go. They are very uncomfortable, in fact they hurt quite a lot, we cannot get out, we're trapped, just have to wait for it to finish. My back feels bruised, and my legs, I think I would have done less damage falling down a flight of steps. Lesson learnt. Darren is busy chatting to a group of men, they are bodyguards travelling from one venue to another. Eventually the time passes and we clamber onto the train. It's a bit too cold to sleep properly, but we doze a little. Subsequently we are transferred to a bus, a boat and another bus, this time squashed with luggage all on top of everyone.

Monday 18th....Arrive at 11am and jump in a taxi to Sanur beach, this is supposed to be the quiet side of the island, we shall see. After travelling slowly on roads that are choked with cars, we finally arrive. We find a nice room, in a home stay, almost on the beach. £25 a night not bad, the hotels are charging hundreds!!!!

Tuesday 19th.   Beach, swim, eat.....it's gorgeous. Soft white beach, warm sea, plenty of shops and places to eat. We meet a guide name of Rino. For a bottle of beer, (this being his main, if not only diet) he will sort out any excursions we want to go on. He's a really interesting friendly guy, whom we all like and enjoy spending time with. Originally from Borneo, he limps because of an old motorbike injury, he sleeps on the beach, and smiles all the time. He has some great stories to tell.

Wednesday 20th..   Through the internet, we learn that, James is going to arrive in Brisbane on the 6th May so we book our ticket for the 29th April leaving here at 12.10am and arriving in AUSTRALIA at 8am. We will need a few days to sort out the paperwork, and to find the port.

Thursday 21st... I aking a walk along a street, just one road back from the beach, and we come across another homestay. We decide to check it out, and it was worth it, it's half the price of the first one. O.K. not on the beach, but it has a great balcony, with chairs, and plenty of places to eat at a stones throw away.

 Friday ---Beach, swim, eat.

Saturday, we go on a day trip and visit a volcano, arranged by Rino, and we have a good look around a few towns. We visit the famous monkey forest, they are everywhere, they jump onto peoples shoulders and steal hats or sunglasses, or whatever they can get. It's amusing as long as it's not you. One of the big males takes a dislike to us. Darren has to chase him away, he gets pretty vicious, but Darrens' boot wins the argument. After that I wasn't sorry to leave.

  Beach, sea, eat, bed........

Sunday and Monday- Same, same, it's a hard life haha!

Tuesday 26th......We go fishing in the morning, again, all arranged by Rino, of course. The sea was calm and beautiful, the boat had a glass bottom so we could see all the beautiful coral. The first to catch a fish was Beverley, (the vegetarian) - a trigger fish - and it was the largest, we caught over 20 between us. It was a lot of fun.

 Back to the beach and walking up and down the esplanade. We have done this countless times in the last few days. The people are calling out to us constantly "transport sir maam, - I give your special price -- lucky price -- morning price ---remember me, you promised to buy from me " it goes on and on and they try to make you feel guilty, but of course there are others who are really cheerful and chatty without the hype, it's all part of it.

In the evening we have the fish we caught, cooked on the seafront and share with our friend and guide Rino, and a French lady and an Italian lady, who we had met up with, a wonderful day to remember!

Wednesday 27th,,,,, we fly tomorrow !!

Thursday 10.30 am. The 28th. Off with Rino and his driver to Kuta beach. This is the main holiday beach and town. As we walk, we see where the Bali bombing took place, and we visit the memorial ,so sad. This town is a lot bigger and busier than where we stayed, I think we all prefer where we were.

After that up to airport for 3pm. We sit and read our books. The desks open at 10pm. I think we must of visited all the airport shops a dozen times, but it passed the time away. Everytime I think about the flight my stomach goes into knots. I love it, the excitement is brilliant. I do hope we like Australia, after all this, hope so....

Friday 29th 12.30 am and we take off. This is it, there is no going back now, floods of nagging questions attack my energized brain. Should we have stayed in France, or gone back to live in England? Our families are so far away, we will ever see them again? All these questions, I am so eager to get things right. My stomach rolls and I realise how excited and happy I am, and looking at Beverley and Darren I can see they are too. It's time to rest, while we can, before the big Australian adventure starts.

We all grabbed a few hours sleep and landed –In Brisbane Australia. Is this real, is it   actually happening, we've made our dream come true. My heart is pounding, I am so proud of us, what a family, I want to shout it out loud and tell everyone. I allow myself a big cheesy grin across my face, take a few deep breaths and here we go!!!!! It is 6.30am our time, 8.30am local time

First impressions -

People are polite, helpful and seem to be generally pleased with life.

Me and Beverley head off to the toilet. This is exciting, after such a long time, how clean will it be? We enter the cleanest, proper toilet imaginable - even the taps are connected, and no drain smells - what a treat, we both shout out loud "yes", and jump up and down. We receive some humorous glances, but we have all just come off the same flight so I think they understand, who cares!

Then it's straight to immigration. All our information is on the computer, the visa details all perfectly correct, passports stamped, and we're in, so easy. What a relief, I've had dreams of arriving at immigration and them having no records. I guess I'm not up to date with the computer world, well I have been living in the depths of the countryside in rural France.

We jump onto a train to the centre of Brisbane to, what appears to us, but probably is not, a very high-class backpacker area. Everywhere is so clean, including the air, I love this place.

 In the main the people are taller than they have been for a time. Taller and a larger size - I feel like a size 8, and that's not strictly true!

It's warm, and after a short shower there is a smell of wet cut grass, how wonderful.

 We go to eat, and find a small café selling chips, pies and many delicious items that we have missed. It is very, very expensive, but expected. Then we book into a backpackers place called Chill. To us, it's like a 4 star hotel, except the bedroom is a bit tight to move around in. It has a huge kitchen for everyone to share. There are burners, ovens, sinks, all the utensils and plates you could need, fridges, tea towels, just everything. Outside there is an eating area, tables chairs, outside swimming pool of course, and magnificent views over the city.

A trip to the supermarket follows. We are like three little children in a toy shop at Christmas, all the shelves are full of scrumptious , mouth-watering delights. We buy thick sliced bread and crumpets and salad and veggie burgers and eat and eat---- ooh western food   -- loving it all!

Sat 30th…..Shopping again, this time for Darren, to buy trousers and shoes as he only has his Bali T shirt and shorts with flip flops. We find Woolworths it's great!!   Lot's of young people are all dressed up for the week-end in all sorts of bizarre outfits, it's fabulous to see, and really good for Beverley, she loves it.

This is a beautiful city with new and old buildings side by side. There are any places to sit and take in the sights, lots of sculptures and parks, we take loads of photos.

In the shops Beverley is back to being her size, that is - age 12 ,- all across Asia, with the people being smaller, she has been an extra large adult size.

There is tons of food for sale which we are just too full to try. Another strange thing for us is the cars, they are all stopping at the red lights, the lights are no longer optional!!

Sunday 1st...Bad night, Beverley has been vomiting and has a rotten temperature, I think it's from the plane, we spend the day in the room. Darren goes out and checks out another backpacker hostel. We move tomorrow to a family room with en-suite, tv and fridge and room to move.

Monday 2nd May .. Beverley much better but weak with very sore tummy muscles. The new room is nicer, and they also have a big clean kitchen, full of young people , it's like a 18-30 party hostel. We notice a bit further up the road a YHA (youth hostel Australia) and check it out....it is even better, we join and get members discount. The price is about the same but there are people of all ages here and feels much more comfortable. No longer wlll we havc to search for rooms as they cover all of Oz....we move again tomorrow....

Tuesday 3rd.. Beverley is better and changing our room goes well. We've only been here a couple of days, but we've learnt a lot already. We go to several banks and choose the National Bank of Australia. We open an account very easily, and find that they also do car insurance, which we take out, that makes life easier. Next we buy a phone card. Darren sorts out an agent to organize importing the car. This is going to cost, but, it's very complicated and we figure that the cost of travelling in taxis and trains going to the port and back, would also be expensive, so we will let someone else do it, for a change!

Wednesday 4th...The papers we need have not arrived at the DHL office? Darren goes to see Colin, our agent, he finds out that James is already here, he arrived on the 3rd - we were told the 6th. This means there is a huge rush on to get him out of dock before the port charges start, you get 3 free days while the paperwork is sorted, we really are glad we have an agent now, it's all in his hands......

Thursday 5th May...8 o'clock and we are off to Australia Zoo, (Steve Irwin- crocodile hunter). It's a one hour train ride and then a free bus transfer to the zoo. We see girls and boys in school uniforms, the boys who, some of which, must be at least sixteen are wearing shorts, you would never see that in France, or England. The youngsters give up seats to the adults, you wouldn't see that either, it's great to see, love this country.

 We have a fabulous time, the zoo is immaculate, the animals are all in proper environments with plenty of space, they are happy, (non of this pacing up and down that we've seen in Asia). The place is so clean it's untrue---we feed and stroke kangaroos and see koalas, we have a photo taken with Beverley holding a koala. She soon learns that they are not as cuddly as you would think -- as she holds it, it's claws scratch her around the waist and on her shoulder, it poos into her hands and scent marks her with its chest onto her T shirt, all this time looking adorable. She smells like extraordinarily strong cat pee, we go and buy her a new T shirt. Then we do the rest of the zoo, including seeing the croc show.......It was an, almost, perfect day out, back to hostel about 5.30pm.

Fri-Sat-Sunday 8th May 2011..........Looked around the town awaiting news of James----We go over the bridge to the South Bank, the river (and everywhere) is very clean. Past the big wheel and open air theatre in a walkway completely covered in purple bougainvillea, so beautiful. There are many market stalls, it begins to cool down which gives me a good reason to buy Beverley a very fashionable cardigan. There are lots of restaurants and cafes, we buy chips in paper--ooh so good. We see free to use bbq's everywhere, and watch -on the street- magic shows, we visit the museum, which was fascinating, we see the night lights in the city, really extraordinarily beautiful.

Mon-Tues-Wed 11th...Car problems--now, apparently, the car belongs to DHL because we used that as our mailing address, never heard such rubbish, the papers all have to return to Malaysia before we can continue, we have the feeling that someone is stalling for time, we continue to discover Brisbane---still love it!!!!

Thursday 12th----Darren phones Colin and says he has had enough, and wants to go to the port himself and sort out customs face to face. Surprise, surprise, Colin jumps (our plan is working) he says he will get onto it and will phone us back....At 1pm we learn we have an appointment at 1.30pm with AQIS - the quarantine people---we jump into a taxi and rush to meet Colin. Mo and Beverley have to wait at the office as there is no room in Colins' car for us......1 hour later Darren is back with James, amazing, seems our hunch was correct.

Friday 13th......166313.....Back on the road again!!! 9am leaving Brisbane on our way to Wauchope, near Port Macquarie, about half way to Sidney - 567km. We have had to rush this part of the coast to meet up with Paul, whom we met in Mongolia, before he leaves on another adventure.

At 10.20am we leave Queensland and enter New South Wales. We fill up with diesel, there are petrol stations but the next 24hr station is 127km away. We see cattle and miles of sugar cane, pass through Sugar Town and Dead Mans Creek, such wonderful names. We see our first signs for kangaroos, but haven't seen any wild ones yet. Half way we stop for a cup of tea and see brightly coloured parrots, they are so gorgeous, seems untrue watching flocks above us----at 4.10pm we see our first 3 kangaroos, this also seems unreal.

5.30pm and we arrive at Pauls, he makes us so welcome, and asks us to stay as long as we want, he cooks us a meal and makes up beds, Peter from Denmark arrives, we also met him in Mongolia. Then follows a superb evening with lots of chatting, storytelling and a few beers--of course!!!!

Saturday 14th...Sitting on the porch, in the hot sun, meeting some of Pauls friends. He shows us his cars, he has about 9 old Toyota Land Cruisers. We go to local shops to buy dinner, and beer for tonight, (our turn). The prices are a good deal cheaper here. We take a drive around Port Macquarie and visit Town beach, it is stunning, and not a piece of rubbish to be seen. There are kangaroos and koalas all over the place. I'm beginning to believe that we are in Australia.

Our evening is spent chatting about Australia, the different towns and cities. Paul teaches us so much, he is a 7th generation Ozy, that meaning his forefather was a so called criminal. He also fought in Vietnam and has travelled the world, and gained an astonishing amount of interesting and useful information. Again he puts the idea of Broome to us, we say we thought it might be a bit small, he agrees but says that will only be for a short while as it is growing so fast and now is the time to invest in land and property. I think Broome is possibly back on ....

Sunday 15th....10.30am, we are packed and off to Tamworth. Darren was born in the English Tamworth and then we can say we drove from one to the other.

It's a beautiful sunny day and the sky is so blue --we drive through rainforests along windy roads up and over the mountains to the plains. We see parrots of the most staggering vivid colours. We pass many creeks and different areas called shires, which makes me think of Bilbo Baggins. We see one side of the road orange/yellowy/tan fields and the other side an intense bright green, stunning.

4.40pm and we arrive at Tamworth - the home of country music and famous for a huge model of a guitar, (no comment). We find a lovely cosy motel with everything you could want, except wifi, never mind, can't have everything. The motel is run by a very friendly Scottish couple who tell us that coming to Australia was the best move anyone could ever make! We will take a rest here for a couple of days......

Monday 16th....We go shopping and buy a tent, sleeping bags, beds, table and chairs, pillows and pillowcases. It is lovely to think that nobody else has slept on them – they are ours!!!! We know it can get cold here at night as the winter comes, we'll see how it goes.

Tuesday 17th...166824....9am passing through Scone and Aberdeen on our way to Newcastle and the coast road south. Have just passed a sign that said Brisbane 839km. wow!

Wednesday 18th....167000....Camping, beaches, parrots, it's lovely and warm, we meet an Irish couple who have been here for years, and they, like everyone we meet, are friendly and tell us we have done the right thing coming to Oz, they love it.

Thursday 19th....167004.....9.30am off to Sydney---11.30--wow--this is one big city, there are 4.6 million people living here. Nobody takes any notice of James, they are all just too laid back "no worries". We drive over Harbour Bridge and on to the Opera House---hard to believe this is real. There is underground car parking for the Opera House but James is too tall. Consequently we take a chance and drive up to an entrance. We stop and the chap says " Sorry no vehicles allowed past this point," so Darren explains we cannot park and have driven all this way could we just drive up to the front for a few piccies. The answer was "No worries mate, help yourself"--- what a country!! Then off we go to Bondi Beach (about 12.50pm). we park - have a cup of tea, I buy a couple of postcards, well you have to at a place like this! A walk on the beach, wonderful.

1.40pm back on the road, passing signs for Liverpool as we head for Wollongong........stopping for some fish and chips, ---there are plenty of fish and chip shops and a Woolworths in every town. Beverley says she still cannot believe she is in Oz, and I agree, we have seen and done so much, and so quickly! As we eat our food, sitting on a bench, there are white parakeets walking around and helping themselves to our chips.

We find a good campsite and notice that it is the same price for a pitch with or without electricity. We go and buy a new light and an electric heater---shear luxury.......we book in for 2 nights....

Fri 20th,,,,167167......Up and make tea using our kettle and toaster. I find it satisfying to have your own things, to know where they have been. Darren doesn't get this at all.

Off to the trailer shop, we are told it is just down the road only 50=60km. In a country so massive 50km is just around the next bend. We find it, but after chatting to the helpful, friendly people in the shop, we learn that you have to register a trailer at your home address. So we cannot buy one, shame, our idea was to sort out our space problem, whilst stopping Darren having to climb up and down the roof of the Landy fighting with tarpaulins. Also we might have been able to start collecting bits and pieces for our house, never mind. Instead we buy a new big, thick tarpaulin and put some things on James' roof , to make room for all the camping equipment.

While driving we see signs for wombats crossing. Unfortunately the only one we see didn't quite make it. Sad, but it gave us the chance of an interesting close up look.

Sat 21st.....167264...... It's a lovely warm day, sitting on the beach at Shell harbour, running (slowly in my case) up and down the sand dunes, glorious. We see 2 weddings on the beach aahhhh!

Sunday 22nd May 2011......167282.............On the road to Batemans Bay, it's another sunny day with clear blue skies. We take an off road detour on a dirt track through part of a National Forest, there are dozens of kangaroos. It's so exhilarating,,, this is what we have been hoping to see. It's a strange sight to see so many of them, just doing whatever it is kangaroos do, staring at us as we pass. The forest becomes very thick, the track takes us back to the main road.

We stop for fish and chips, buy a fishing rod for Darren and a hand reel for Beverley, find a camp site and go fishing, we catch nothing.

Mon 23rd......167395.......Up early on our way to Eden, we stop along the way at Bermagui to find a campsite and fishing pitch. A dazzling sea view from the tent. Perfect fishing spots on the rocks amongst the glorious sandy beaches. Sitting here writing I have a purple flowering cacti next to me. It's autumn here and cooling down enough for a jacket as the sun goes down. Otherwise you can tell by the bright red and oranges of the European trees, the native trees don't seem to be shedding at all. We meet a couple from Melbourne, who are driving upwards for the winter, they tell us that Western Australia is even more beautiful than this.....how can it be?..

Tuesday 24th....Went fishing today at a lake and caught nothing. Then we spotted a bakery and re-discovered steak and kidney pies and veg pasties, we ate two each! Fishing in the sea at Camel Rock and we caught a Bream, we took a walk to rock pools, the water is so clean and clear. Then back to the tent and cooked the fish on the bbq, gorgeous, ---- we all listen to music, play cards and Sims---bed.........

Wednesday 25th May.....167475.....Up at 6.30am, nice and warm, we left the little fan heater on all night. 9am on the road again

We see flocks of vivid green and red parrots flying overhead against a bright blue sky!!!!! The coastal road is spectacular, we cross crystal clear rivers on wooden bridges and see white beaches with the sun reflecting off the breakers. We go along Mimosa Rocks National Park road through fantastic rainforest. We are on the Princes Highway on the Sapphire Coast.

10.45am We arrive at Eden and drive through to the Victoria border, expecting a fruit fly check. We have no fruit or vegetables in the car, and see nothing except a sign that states no fresh fruit or veg.

It's not very warm now, and raining, but I suppose it is rainforest!!!---We find a lovely campsite by the beach, we set up and then go to explore. It is mind-boggling, as far as you can see in every direction there is no sign of life. It feels really strange -- the beach is 90 miles long, should be enough for a stroll!!!

Thursday 26th May..... We spent the morning fishing, and as usual, caught nothing. At the fishing shop we find out about high tides, and where and when to fish, this should help.

While we are out we meet a lovely dog. He is a cross Malamute husky, called Angel, with one blue and one brown eye and the softest, daft dog temperament, very much like Beau. Should be time to get the tissues out, but I decide to bite my lip instead. I miss my dogs so much it hurts, but they are not my dogs anymore, I gave them away. A quick wish that they are both happy, then stop thinking, change the subject and move on.

Our evening is spent fishing , at high tide as suggested, and we catch a huge salmon. Now we have caught it, we must eat it. So we gut it, clean it, wrap it in foil and throw it on the bbq. So simple, but we make a bit of a mess of it, it's a bit too thick to cook through properly before the foil falls to pieces, but we have learnt a lot, and will know better for next time! We still manage a meal from it, and that's the main thing.

Sitting outside our tent is a beautiful ,bright red and blue parrot. This country is stunning, like England but coloured in === love it!!

Friday 27th May......167690......Off at 9.45am and heading towards Melbourne.

.Thinking of my brother today as it is his birthday, I do miss him, thoughts of family flood into my mind.I tell myself that we are so fortunate to be here, in an attempt to stop sad feelings,

We pass through Stratford, and yes it is on the river Avon. Then through Sale, where we stop for lunch, and shop for bits for the tent. We buy an electric light and a hairdryer, (ooh luxury), a couple of cheap plastic tool boxes, one for fishing bits and one for Beverley to put all her drawing materials in. For the car, new brushes for the alternator, hope it works.

We pass through Trafalgar with its grey skies and rain. Supposed to be 2" of rain in May, nobody mentioned it all fell on the same day!!!   I phone ahead to the YHA (hostel) in Melbourne and book a room, no camping tonight------3.50 the rain stops and it's sunny---we see a sign "Welcome to Melbourne" we are back in four lane traffic, moving very slowly, accident ahead!!   We arrive safely at YHA, again a lovely clean place, nice room, kitchen, television room etc.., we meet a Thai lady traveller and spend an hour or so swapping stories......

Saturday 28th May....167882......In the morning with grey skies, we go onto the roof terrace of the YHA to take photos of Melbourne. It could be any city, nothing stands out, just the same old buildings, reminds us very much of Birmingham, so we decide to not bother with photos....

9.25am. Off to Torquay and the start of the 125 mile long Great Ocean Road. It runs right on the coastline, it was built by ex-servicemen after WW1 in homage to comrades killed. It is said to be one of the worlds' best drives......exciting!!!

1.15pm. With skies clearing, we arrive and go to Bells beach, apparently known as "home of the rip curl" a famous surfing spot. It's absolutely stunning with at least 30 people in the water, surfing!!!!! This is the Australia that we have seen on t.v.

Next stop Anglesea, as we drive it's just one beautiful bay after another, mind boggling. We stop to look at a lighthouse, then we decide not to bother to walk to it, will probably have to pay and its only a lighthouse...

Then onto Lorne, we stop at Irskine falls, but we have seen lots of bigger waterfalls.

With comments like "decide not to bother" and "seen lots of bigger waterfalls", I believe we are starting to get very tired, maybe it's time to stop travelling, not far to Bunbury !

We drive through beautiful rainforest (just like in Laos) -- we see dozens of white parakeets and pink and grey parrots. I think they are digging for worms after the rain, either that or they have learnt to line dance. Flying overhead we see purple, red and blue parrots--wow!! Still in Lorne, a very picturesque sea-side town, with a pier. The sun breaks through and the sea changes from grey to turquoise green to bright blue, amazing the difference a little sun can make, the white surf sparkles as it bubbles up the beach, Beverley says it looks like snow.....

Sunday 29th May....We have stopped at a camp site at Skenes Creek, just 5km short of Apollo Bay. We are separated from the beach by sand dunes and bushes, with narrow paths leading straight through. We have electric, the showers and toilets are ok, although possibly the oldest and tattiest we have seen. It starts as a quiet day, sunny in morning, rainy in afternoon. We get chatting to Charlie who leases and runs this place, he also buys and sells caravans, and wants to re-build the showers and toilets. Before we know it, we have bought a caravan, (3800 dollars) which will be partly paid for by Darren working!!!!! This will hold our travelling up for about 2 to 3 weeks. After living in the car and rentals, the caravan is huge. It has a double bed at one end, with a sliding door, for privacy, (what's that?). Also a kitchen-come sitting room, with a table and a pull down settee for Beverley, which is full bed length and only 4" off the size of a double, and as for storage---it's a TARDIS!!!—Luxury!!!

Monday 30th----to----Friday 3rd June.......We have moved into the caravan, no shock there! The weather has got colder, but it's still bright and sunny. We have spent our time walking and playing on the beach with Chloe, Charlies' dog. Leaning against a tree we found a pile of rusty old bikes. Charlie let us help ourselves to three of them, they are a bit corroded but they work, and good fun, haven't ridden a bike since Laos.!!!!

Darren is busy ripping out the old showers, happy to be working. He has been offered 6 months work by the local plumber, good pay etc., but we decide to decline, it's beautiful here, but again it's too quiet and not what we have come here for.............Perth is calling. Darren, on the other hand, would quite happily stay here, as he would of done in many places we have passed through, the Land Rover garage in Malaysia for one.

Me and Beverley have been thinking about getting a dog, just a little one. We did promise her one, once we had somewhere to live, and now we have the caravan.

Saturday 4th June...The caravan is now home and feels cozy and secure after the tent. Lovely, just a dog missing, so off we go to the dog rescue at Geelong, about 2 hours away, we look for a small dog. Perhaps the cross sausage dog that we spotted. We make enquiries and are told that all dogs have at least a two week wait and cost 275dollars, not really what we had in mind. We go buy some chips and I buy the local paper - and see "Cross husky and American staff, short hair, 2yrs old boy- neutered and vac. 2 blue eyes---FREE to good home" Unable to resist we go to visit. His name is Boomer, his coat is the colour of a golden Labrador, he has a white mark on his neck in the shape of a boomerang, he is a proper dog, eats everything and doesn't pull on the lead----we are all very happy with him! That didn't take us long to sort out, it's a good feeling to have him with us.

Sun-Mon 5th+6th June.....walking Boomer, riding bikes around camp site------Boomer decides he wants to join us bike riding, he slips his collar and comes bounding along, wide eyed, looking very proud of himself, he is no problem and stays with us.

The weather is beginning to get much colder....

Tuesday 7th...Rain storms and hail, just inland from us there is snow, it doesn't settle but it's still there!!! Are we too far south? On chatting to the locals, it seems this is normal winter weather ----according to our guide book this area only has a couple of inches of rain per month. After thinking about it , this is obviously ridiculous as we are surrounded by acres and acres of rainforest, it is not what we expected, we are learning so much, it makes it more exciting and makes us more aware of the countryside around us, (and makes me yearn for the warmth of W.A).

Darren still has a couple of days work to do and on Friday the caravan should be registered in our name. Charlie has let us use his address to register it and is helping us with all the details, it's very good of him.

This week-end is the Queens birthday, it's a big thing here. It is a long week-end, the campsites are full and the shops are closed, so we will probably hang on till early next week........

Wednesday 8th....Raining with bits of blue sky...8am we take Boomer for his morning stroll on the beach, the waves are huge—scary. Then we find proof that we are too far south, we find a dead penguin on the beach, we are a hundred miles south of Tasmania, how cold is it there?

Today Darren is putting shelves up in the caravan, even more space! If ever the caravan feels a little cramped, when we are climbing over each other, we just say the magic word "TENT" and it's huge again!!!!

Thursday 9th.......We drive an hour to Colac town, to buy the electric brake parts for the caravan/car. It's a lot warmer now, with sunny intervals. We buy Boomer a squeaky ball and it's a winner, he loves it and carries it around squeaking contentedly. This is the only sound we have heard from him, apart from a loud yawn, he doesn't bark even when confronted with the campsites cat......

 Friday 10th to Monday 13th June 2011. Cleaning and preparing the caravan for the road----still cold but sunny----found another penguin on the beach.

Tuesday 14th.....168510..... Charlie and Kev, who lives in a caravan on site, help us with the final preparations. We say our goodbyes, and we are off on the Great Ocean Road towards Warnambool. It feels good to be moving again and to leave Skeynes Creek, a very beautiful, but much too quiet a place for me !

 We pass through National parks and see the limestone sculptures created by the sea called the 12 apostles. Loch Ard gorge with its ship wreck story , the Arch, London Bridge, the Grotto, they are all stunning views. We read on the placards, that in the time of sailing ships, there were 80 shipwrecks off this coast in 40 years. We stop at a site at

Peterborough, the brakes on the caravan are not working and we need two new tyres . We will slowly make our way to Warnanbool tomorrow. Boomer is behaving, he's no trouble in the car and in the caravan he plays with his toys, and us, and has us all laughing. Beverley is content, at last she has someone else to talk to besides us.

Wednesday 15th......168584........Off at 10am with sun and blue skies, it's a bit fresh, but ok. We arrive at Warnabool and find a lovely clean site, with spotless showers and toilets with fresh flowers, a definite improvement.

Darren takes off the caravan wheels and we take them to a garage for new tyres. Then off to K mart to buy (really cheap) new kettle as the one we have scalds us each time we use it, not good. A new toaster, with our present one, we have to hold the button down all the time it's on, and then it only toasts one side. Next, an oil filled radiator, Charlie had leant us one and we have got spoiled and used to it. An electric grill/oven and a DS game for Beverley, feels like Christmas. Then it's back to our beach side caravan site, not such a hard life. On site we shower, then stay in our nice warm caravan , this is much better than camping!!!!!

Thursday 16th....Boomer is running free on the beach, he responds very well to treats, seems very trainable. At the site we meet Don and Sharon and Frank and his wife, they are very friendly people and take Darren fishing with them. Again he has no luck, but has enjoyed himself.

Friday 17th.......168651....Preparing to move, and the bracket holding the (new) jockey wheel snaps and the caravan hits the floor, no damage but yet another repair for Darren to do!----10.45am off to Port Fairy, through Dartmoor.

At 1.55pm we enter South Australia, there is no quarantine stop, just a sign and a bin for fresh fruit and veg. There is nobody there, its works on trust at this crossing. We stop and bin half an onion and a cabbage, then off to Mount Gambier. The sun comes out as we cross the border.....we drive on to a town called Millicent, through miles and miles of straight roads, it's very green and very flat, good for towing. This is a forestry area with lots of logging. We find another great caravan park. Beverley rides around the camp on her rusty old bike, Boomer sits with me watching every move she makes. Next to us, on the site, are two very friendly couples, retired and living on the road. It seems to be very common to retire and travel around this beautiful country. They are all known as the grey nomads, brilliant!

Saturday 18th.......

We arrive at Robe, a very pretty seaside town. At the first caravan site, we find a delightful beach but there are no people here, even the reception is on the end of a phone, just too quiet. The second site there are a few grey nomads, we settle in and spend the day - quiet - stunning cliffs and beach. Boomer loves it, Beverley takes him to the beach and he tries to catch a crab, so funny to watch him playing. We have, yet another go at fishing, no joy. Time to move on again.

Sunday 19th June 2011..............168842.....10am on the road towards Adelaide 336km away, the first town we pass will be Kingston SE. It rained in the night, sunny now and definitely warmer. On the long straight roads, we see rabbits, parrots, and another wombat (dead again).

 Boomer is asleep across my lap, as usual. He is excellent in the car, and in the caravan, and with other dogs, and people, he is good on the lead, and eats anything. I think we may have dropped lucky with this one!!!!

 We see hundreds of sheep with new born lambs and acres and acres of vineyards. One I notice is called Murdup wine, I wonder if that is well known, I have no idea!

Arriving at Kingston SE we see "Larry the lobster" a huge plastic tourist attraction, looks a bit sad to me. On to Salt Creek, which is made up of a roadhouse come petrol station, and has a population of about two. Then onto Miningie which is in the Coorong national park. We see sand-dunes, salt lagoons and huge flying pelicans, wow.... in places it reminds me of Khazakstan.

Monday 20th June.....169002.....WE arrive at Adelaide Hills, a beautiful area, in places there are dozens of European trees glowing in their autumn colours. Arrival at Adelaide city brings us a problem, we cannot get on the beach site with Boomer. We soon find a nice dog friendly site called Windsor Gardens, lesson learnt, things have changed now we have a Boomer. We take a drive around the city and the suburbs, seems a really attractive city, but still a city! Back on site, and we are warned that tonight is going to be the worst storm that they have seen for two years, and to batton down the hatches, and all that. We have no idea how bad these storms can be, it certainly sounds bad. In the end we only got a little rain and some winds.

Tuesday 21st.....169080.....10am sunny, and off towards Port Augusta, as we leave Adelaide it becomes very flat and desert like. We see what is called outback art, huge metal statues of insects, spaceships and all sorts of different things, it's really good! ---- 11am passing through Dublin, we see Alpacas for sale, thousands more sheep and wind farms, and a train, even longer than the ones in China. We arrive at Port Pirie, then a little further - 20km - to Port Germain for a site on the beachfront.......it is so quiet here. They have a post office/store, a hotel/pub which is open 12-2 and 6-8, the caravan park, and a police station, with a police car that doesn't move, and at night the station is lit up by fairy lights, the only thing that's missing is people!!!

Wednesday 22nd June 2011 ..... Returned to Port Pirie for supplies and the half shaft welding (which we had done in Thailand - Satun) it has finally broken, Darren had been expecting this. Trudging around town asking if anyone could weld it, four garages we tried, they were all capable of doing the job, but just couldn't seem to comprehend what we wanted, and to be honest didn't seem to want to know. At the fifth garage we met Sam the welder, he was the first person to understand what we wanted, and all was fixed in a very short while. Next we went to the cycle shop for a new handlebar for my bike, as the one it has is a racing version, and it's not very comfy for me, I prefer to sit upright when cycling. Also we needed new brake cables for Beverleys' bike.

Thursday 23rd.....We have stayed an extra day, to walk the one mile long, longest pier in the Southern Hemisphere, so we have been informed. We have ridden our bikes, it's now so warm we are back in our T. shirts. Boomer is running free up the beach and into the shallow sea, looking very pleased with himself.

Friday 24th June.....169266...Off at 9.45am, back to see Sam to weld the safety towing chains to the caravan, a good job done in minutes for only 20 dollars, thank you Sam.

I have just read, that here in South.Australia, there is a cattle station, in the outback, 34,000 sq km, that is larger than Great Britain, this is one big place!!!

11.30am we pass 169325km which equals 30,000 miles, not bad.

We arrive at Port Augusta we see a sign for Perth W.A, but we don't take it because we have decided to go around the Eyre peninsula, it's not much further, so we turn towards Whyalla. We find a lovely site, again on the beach. Our time is spent cycling around the caravan park trying to wear Boomer out.

Saturday 25th....Apparently this place gets 300 days a year of sunshine, we decide to stay another day. Beverley spends hours embroidering, while watching the box set of Frasier, she loves it. In the afternoon it's 18 degrees and we go fishing, the normal catch of nothing, but we see three dolphins swimming in the marina, what a magnificent sight, another wish granted.....

After dark we watch a film,which was filmod very close to here, "Priscilla Queen of the desert" very witty, and we learn from it, that a town is only a proper town if it has a F***ing Kmart, love it!

Sunday 26th June.....169452.....Off at 9.30am to Cowell, just 108k to a caravan site called Harbour View, hoping for some fishing. 12.30pm, we spot an emu at the side of the road, another reminder of where we are. Here , there are no buildings, just bushes and small trees. The tree trunks and the branches look dead with large bunches of leaves perched on the top, like hats....There are miles and miles of white sandy beaches, and the most magnificent sand dunes, as far as you can see. Just to put the cream on the cake, there are flocks of colourful budgies.

I cannot count how many times on this trip, that I have had the feeling of being so fortunate to see so much of this astonishing world.

Monday 27th......We stay another day to re-visit the sand dunes, can't get enough of them. Boomer is running up and down the dunes with Beverley, then he runs off into the sea and Beverley rolls down the dunes, fantastic, just so beautiful here.......we see many kangaroos and a 8-10 inch dark green skink.

Tuesday 28th...169598....... Off at 9.30am to Port Lincoln, the southern end of the peninsula, it's said to be home of the Tuna fish. The landscape looks lighter , the colour of straw. Miles and miles of straight roads, very flat, thousands of sheep, then suddenly green fields. We arrive at the caravan park around midday, right on the beach by the pier, we try fishing-nothing again. At this port you can cage dive to see the great white sharks or swim with the dolphins and sea lions, bit too cold at the moment!!!

Wednesday 29th....One more go at fishing with the usual result......

Thursday 30th June.....169748......Woken by rain, it's much cooler. Off at 10.20am to Elliston passing through Coffin Bay, love the name. Here there are miles and miles of white rocks and sandy desert with thousands of dead trees. We are now on the Great Australian Bight.

We find a caravan park which is separated from the beach by sand-dunes, we try fishing again, we're not going to give up!

Friday 1st July 2011,,,,,169853......Off at 9.45 towards Ceduna, which is only 468 km from the WA border. The temperature is rising, the newspaper says 24 degrees for this afternoon. We are fighting a strong wind against us, and therefore getting about 12 miles to the gallon!! Arriving at Ceduna and the caravan site is almost full. We ask about fishing and are told to go 12km down the road, why is it never where we are? We decide not to bother. We see a sign stating that cars will not be allowed into WA if they carry soil contamination, therefore we give it a wipe down and decide against any off roading and to stay on the highway, on the blacktop.

Saturday 2nd July ...169990.....We are getting ready for the crossing of the Nullabor Plain--(Nullabor meaning no trees).

Ceduna to the W.A. border is now just 480km

At 11am, we arrive at Penang, a small place that calls itself "The gateway to the Nullabor" We see a sign -- next 79km look out for kangaroos and wombats.....

12.30pm we enter the Yalata Aboriginal Reserve, the landscape is flat and green with miniature trees. The signs for roadtrains are warning us of the danger of their enormous size, we have been advised to just get out of the way! The quarantine inspection is in 300km. Therefore today and tonight we need to eat all our fruit and veg, our guide also says cheese, which we have a lot of......no worries Boomer will help. Boomer has to stay on the lead across the Nullabor, because there is poison bait put down for the dingos and also people keep telling us he looks just like a dingo and if seen running----bang!!!!!!!

12.45pm. We pass over a cattle grid , through the dog fence (which is 5800km long --the dog fence not the cattle grid). This is it Boomer----dingo country!!!

The sat nav says we need to turn right in 995km, ok we'll look out for that!

 Another sign " next 92km - kangaroos—wombats, and camels".

12.55pm another sign "enjoy the whales" because we are getting close to the head of the bight, if we are lucky we may see some whales with their calves, hope we are!

Now the landscape is greeny, blue scrub and sand dunes, we see yellow flowers, maybe early spring flowers?

 It is 15km to the roadhouse, so we decide to set up and come back to see the whales....2.35pm we arrive at roadhouse/caravan site, we have electricity but no running water, not that it matters, we can cope. ...

3.15 Off to whale watch, this is so exciting. There are walkways and viewing points, we see a mother and calf swimming close inshore. " Mon Dieu , mon Dieu" as my friend and French neighbour used to say. This is the most magnificent sight, the sea, the cliffs the whales, as we watch we spot another 5 and there are many others a distance away. A terrific experience, hope to repeat it soon!!!!! We buy a soft toy whale for Beverley to put in her bedroom, when she gets one, and she buys me a purple pen, perfect..

Sunday 3rd.....170188,,,,,,,9am and off, only 183km to go, there are countdown markers on the side of the road---9.30am. Not too far away we see a dingo, it's much thinner in the face than Boomer, and prettier ahhhh, shame, but true. I can understand now, why people told us to keep him on the lead. 10am we see a dead dingo at the roadside.

The land has flattened out and the trees have gone, every so often we see the sea on our left. It's 13 degrees in the car....We see roadtrains heading towards us and when they overtake it feels like they are pulling you over towards them, almost sucking you in, they are huge and fast, very fast.

10.30am sign WA 90km, We see many birds of prey swooping in the air, fantastic to see. There are posts along the road where people have stolen the signs for a souvenir.

I suddenly remember we have fresh garlic in the fridge door, we arrive at the border and I confess, and dutifully hand over the garlic, that's all we have. They quickly check the car and we pass through. The mileage reads 170294---we are now in the Shire of Dundas.

The road drops down onto what used to be the sea-bed and on our right we see the cliffs, now green and covered in shrubs --the trees are back again. Lunch stop at Mundrabilla then onto Mandura….

3.15pm we pass a tree with many hats hanging off it, then we see a teddy bear tree, well that's different. The wind is against, us slowing us down. There is sign for an airstrip on the road ahead, we check the skies but nothing in sight. The road starts to rise up again and we come up off the sea bed. We arrive at the roadhouse and there is a warning poster " beware of snakes and wild dogs", my translation is – if possible do not leave the caravan.

Monday 4th July.....170405, ...Darren rides his bike with Boomer pulling the bike, to exercise him and wear him out a bit, he needs it....8.30am off, we see another decorated tree, this time it's shiny material and socks....it's very cold we can see our breath. New sign for kangaroos , cattle and camels. The land is very flat with every possible shade of green and every shape of bush and trees that, to me, look like giant brocolli, really beautiful...9.15 and we see an emu....9.45am we pass Cocklebiddy Roadhouse. Next is Calguida another 65km. Abruptly the landscape changes, there is nothing, literally nothing but bush for the next 247km before Balladonia-------10.20am arrive Calguida. There is a sign for the Western Time Zone, we turn our clocks back 45 minutes.

Then another sign, the longest stretch of straight road in Oz. 90 miles of blue sky!!

12 midday and the first bend in road. Now the bush is going bluey, green and the earth is orange, it starts to rain. Another airstrip on the road, there's nothing in the sky. We have lunch at Balladonia and carry on...1.30 see some crazy cyclists,,,,,2,20pm pass the Fraser Roadhouse and the largest Eucalyptus forest in Oz. Onto Norseman....2.45 raining again, trees are getting taller, the sand is orange and there are huge areas of it with nothing growing.

We are making good time tucked up behind a roadtrain,,,,,3.15pm we see powerlines then dozens of road side adverts-----We have crossed the Nullabor!!!!!!!!!! Long day today, over 300miles!!!!!!!!!!!!!!!!!!!!

Tuesday 5th.....8.45am and off to the goldmines!! Through Coolgardie and onto Kalgoorlie Boulder-167km, the gold capital of Australia---now with a huge super pit.

The roads are straight with bush on both sides, a railway track on our left, there is rubbish along the side of the road, not a massive amount but the first we've seen since arriving in Oz......We see rough roads leading to mines...yellow warning signs for roadtrains entering and turning and to be careful overtaking. There are more teddy bear trees. We pass Kalgoorlie nickel smelter and on to a caravan site.

Now it's time to go to visit Brian and his wife, whom Darren met on Landyzone, on the internet. What a very freindly couple, he and his wife Charmagne live with three dogs and I don't know how many Landrovers, they are everywhere. James has oil leaks on both front wheels and needs two callipers. Brian has just what we need. Brian works as a prison officer and says that there is loads of work in this area that Darren could do.

Wednesday, Thursday 6th and 7th July.....Darren goes to Brians to sort parts, me and Beverley stay at the caravan park, at last a bit of time to do loads of things we have on hold!!!!

Later we drive around Kalgoorlie and have a look, it has everything you could want, Darren says he would be happy here, he's found another ' brother'. Personally I don't have such good feelings about the place, and it's not by the sea, wasn't that our dream?

Friday 8th.......170872...off to Esperance....back down to Norseman, past the teddy bear trees, then onto Salmon Gums and Grasspatch (got to be the best names so far).

2.30pm about 50km out of Esperance and all of a sudden we find ourselves out of the bush, to green fields and sheep. We find a site, the town is pleasant and the beaches are white and the sea torquoise, really beautiful....

Saturday 9th.....We wake to find Darrens and my bike stolen, we drive around looking, in the hope they have been dumped, but no joy.

Darren goes to the local hospital for a prescription for his Asma, no problems and there's no charge.

We drive the coastal road, wow its gorgeous scenery.....

Sunday 10th.....171152.......9.30am off to Albany, it's a long way and will take us all day ,but then we shall stop for a couple of days.

After studying the maps and chatting, we have decided to end our coastal run. We are going to cut across the land and head up towards Bridgetown and onto Bunbury. We are all a little woary and think it may be time to settle by the sea. I chose Bunbury as it is famous for its dolphins, has plenty of beaches, and shops, including a K.mart, of course! According to the literature I have read it should have everything we will need for our new life. Expectations are high, fingers crossed it's all that we expect!

Driving out of Albany and Darren spots his bike. It's being ridden by a young aboriginal boy about 16. We pull over and Darren approaches him, the first thing the boy says "Is this your bike?" Darren says "Yes, and your going to take me to the other one aren't you?" The boy explains it's nothing to do with him, it was his mate, Darren offers him 20 dollars if he will take us to the other bike, and says no police, the boy gets into the back of the car with me and Boomer. I think he is very unsure of Boomer, not surprising with the size of him and his two piercing blue eyes. Boomer is sitting on my lap desperately trying to lick the boys face, the boy pulls his hood up and tries to hide, of course Boomer thinks this is a wonderful game. He takes us to the bike - no problems, off we go again really happy to have our bikes back, we were not expecting that!

12.30pm. We see a sign for Malleefowl, have no idea, must google them??? See four emus as we arrive at the caravan park. It's raining, we walk through the park to the beach, it looks like good fishing....we will see.

Monday 11th - Tuesday 12th July 2011.. Enjoying staying at the campsite, walking on the beach. Beverley and me take Boomer for a long cycle ride, I am getting the hang of it now, well he hasn't pulled me off the bike!!! Darren tried fishing again, he caught a salmon, but it was too small, so he threw it back in.

Wed. 13th July.......171537......Sunny weather again, I like this. We meet Joan and Collin, whom we first met on the Nullabor, and another couple we keep bumping into, we are all heading towards Perth. We pass through the Shire of Denmark and the Shire of Manjimup and on to Bridgetown. We find another good campsite, and soon settle in.

We go into town to look for a film, to replace the one that stopped working half way through last night. Entering the video shop we hear French being spoken, within seconds Darren is in full conversation, always enjoying using his French. They are the owners of the shop, a really charming couple. We discover that the shop will not open tomorrow until 11.30am for us to return the films. We were expecting to be on the road for about 9am. Although, to them we are only passing travellers, they decide to trust us with their films, amazing! We offer to buy the films, therefore we can get away early. After a few more minutes chatting we have been invited to dinner tonight and have only paid 10 dollars for 3 films, and that was after insisting we pay something, they tried to just give them to us. Dinner was wonderful, we really have hit it off with these people. They have three lovely children, and live in a gorgeous house, just out of town, on top of a hill with breathtaking views. We must keep in touch. Darren loves Bridgetown, and would settle here without even seeing Bunbury. It is beautiful, very green, it reminds me of where we used to live in France, and the English countryside, but the sea is still calling me….

We are ready to head to Bunbury, and find a site and look for a house to rent and, of course, work. This could well be the end of our travelling,(although we will visit Perth at some point in the near future) so we will cross our fingers for Bunbury being what we hope for……….estimated time of arrival is tomorrow morning about lunch time!!

Driving and we pass the town sign we are here!

There is a campsite overlooking Koombana bay, but not for us, they don't take dogs, that's a shame. A couple of km back from the sea and we find a suitable site. It has everything we need including a laundry with driers. To me this is such a luxury, I haven't had to do the washing in a cold river for a long time, but it's still a thrill to empty a machine of warm dry clothes, so easy. So home base is sorted, next to look for a rented house with a garden. Boomer is no trouble but to be able to leave a door open without thinking of where he is, and other dogs, would be good.

Bunbury is a busy town, in fact it's a city. Plenty of shops to explore, and now we can actually start to buy things for a home and our future, oooh exciting! Space has decided what we can have for nearly two years. and that certainly needs a travellers mind to keep it in order.

Next we go to a rental agency and explain our situation. The young girl on the desk asks us for references, which we do not have. After explaining, and then again, she decides this will be no problem as long as we can pay a substantial amount up front, we agree. Darren asks her to go and check this with her superiors before we go any further, she does and confirms it's ok. Now to find a house. We spend the next few days house hunting, this is fun, Australian houses are something new to us. We have been used to stone walls several metres thick, obviously not needed here. We find one we all like and return to the agency, excited. The same young lady on reception smiles and asks for our references. We remind her of the previous conversation, but she is not willing to go any further without written proof that we have been good clients, and have Australia references. Well that was a complete waste of time, not to mention the disappointment, oh well, try again.

Another agency and they have said yes to us, maybe they have a house that is not renting. I have my suspicions that this may be the case.

They have offered us a three bedroom (which we will need as Darrens' mom and dad are going to fly out for a visit), with a garden, not bad, needs a clean and a lick of paint, but is definitely one up from the caravan. Space wise it is huge, and the bathroom and shower are new and clean, yippee, our own bathroom, where we can actually leave things in it….

Our laptop computer is suffering from blackouts, considering what it has been through with all the travelling we cannot complain. The good news is that our other computer (we had in France) is now on its way to us from England, via Darren's mom and dad, plus lots of other goodies and Darren's tools, should be 6 to 8 weeks.

We have been trying to sort out Darrens' many qualifications. Although it took us many hours and pages and pages of proof and references to have them passed by the Australian government, which they did, it now seems that they are worthless unless he retakes them again. This makes sense as to the different rules and regulations out here, the problem is we cannot find anywhere for him to do this. In the meantime he has found himself a job as a roof plumber, for which he doesn't need a 'ticket' as they call it. I guess these are the sort of problems you just cannot see beforehand, luckily he is so versatile.

Apart from problems, Beverley has taken her first (proper) music lesson, I am now a registered home educator and all is going well.

We drove up to Perth today to have a look, it's huge, that's what I call a city, It's beautiful in the centre, but we wouldn't want to live there, too big. Beverley and me love Bunbury, so much to do and enjoy. The down side is that Darren is not happy, he says he prefers Bridgetown, it was gorgeous but no sea, and such a tiny town. Miles from anywhere! What to do?

Looking forward to our nineteen year old nephew flying out to stop with us, he wants to work alongside Darren. Beverley is excited too, it will be wonderful for her to have another young person in the house, instead of just us oldies!

Off to the airport in Perth to await our nephew, so excited! On the drive home we chat about family and what is going on in England, and what our futures may bring in this beautiful country. David is in the third small bedroom, no bed yet, just a mattress on the floor, at least all the bedding is brand new. We can in time get some furniture for him, when we know what he wants. We take him to visit the local animal park, here we can get up close and stroke kangaroos, see all the parrots, and other birds, some of which are tame enough to climb over our shoulders and eat food from our hands. Not the same as seeing them in the wild, but it's an easy introduction, to what lives here. Then to the beach with the openness and space, we are lucky and catch site of some dolphins.

David is very quiet and seems to be worrying deeply about being here, away from the rest of the family and his friends, hope he can settle. He goes off to work with Darren, but it is not what he expected, he is very uncomfortable being on the roof of a house. He doesn't like heights, not his thing. I can understand this, given time he may get used to it, Darren is not so patient and teases him, using his usual saying of 'toughen up princess'. Darren seems to think that this saying is the answer to any situation where he cannot understand someone. Well not this time!

I can hardly believe it, it's just one week later and David has booked his flight back home. There has been lots of discussion and the outcome is that, he does not want to be here. He misses his family and friends too much. It's the wrong time for him, maybe when he is a bit older. The good thing is, that he has realised how happy he was in England, maybe he took it all for granted, as we do, but not now. It may of only been a week but I think he has learnt an awful lot. We will miss him, especially Beverley, they never even got to go out anywhere together. I asked him to stay on for a bit, just as a holiday, but he is not interested in anything but getting back to his friends, and his mom.

Every week-end we are going up to Bridgetown to catch up with our new friends. We have noticed that we do not seem to be making any new friends in Bunbury. Is it because it's a city, or because we are only around when everyone is at school and work, who knows. Well going away every week-end is not helping, there are so many things going on around us but we cannot join in.

The house we are in is fine except that it is on the main road, which is very awkward for Darren, trying to get in and out with his ute and trailer. We really don't like renting, can't do anything to it, also the heating has broken, the agency doesn't care that it is really cold in the morning, and we are not allowed to touch it, so frustrating. Therefore we have been looking at houses to buy and have narrowed the list down to three which we are visiting on Wednesday, then we shall put an offer in, we have a financial broker and all seems ok.

A few months have gone by since I wrote anything. The news is we have bought a house, it's wonderful, all ours.

We have also brought , (from Lucie and Andre) a land cruiser. We had to replace James, no fault of James, but we cannot register him. We entered the country on a temporary carnet (passport) on the advice of the RAC in England. As we were driving across Australia it made James legal to travel from state to state without registering him. The idea was that when we settled we registered, but apparently we do not have the proper import papers to do this. The only way is for James to be shipped out on a boat and brought back in to Perth, the cost of which, and the time it would take, has prevented us from going down that route, James now sits in Lucie and Andres' garden, his zebra stripes blending in with the trees.

Still going away at week-ends and having a great time, with our new friends. Darren is helping them build a new house. Here in Bunbury, we are starting to get to know people.. Beverley and me are out on our bikes most days. There are no hills here and it is made for cyclists. We cycle to the beach and to the main town, the library and find new shops and places all the time.

Darren has bought himself a Triumph Bonneville which is immaculate, it came with a second bike, for spares. He can now enjoy the freedom of the open roads, and lack of traffic, when outside the city, of course, at and around Bridgetown. Job wise, he is not so happy, it is becoming apparent that the future of the company he is with, is not as exciting as we thought. His boss just seems to dream about it, but not put anything into place, it may be time to move on. He has decided to acquire some tickets for fork lift and elevated work platforms, so he can look at work on the mines.

Bridgetown Sunday market, all the local folk selling their produce and wares. So many people who obviously know each other. I have to admit that it's a much friendlier place than Bunbury. I am comparing a country town with a city, what outcome do I expect? Behind one of the craft stalls is a car with its' boot open. A bundle of puppies roll around on the newspaper, all free to good homes. I am so tempted, a buddy for Boomer, a companion for Beverley, it's her birthday in two weeks. Who am I trying to kid, it's the aah factor that has won me over, Will stick to Beverleys' birthday present, because I know she melts when she sees puppies. I am told that the mother of the puppies is a dachshund, I can see that in their short haired pointy snouts. I know Beverley wants a longer haired dog, an Old English sheepdog, to be exact. There sitting at the back of the boot, is the odd one out, the ugly duckling, perhaps. She is gorgeous, quite long curly hair, all colours with a little white beard, obviously doesn't take after her mother, she's the one –aaaaah! We take her home and present her to the sleeping Beverley. At first she thinks it's a joke, her Dad teasing her, with our friends dog, Vesper. When Darren says "surprise" Beverley mutters "I don't want Vesper on my head". I follow up with a "happy birthday" then, the warm puppy breath wakes her up, , and just like her mother she says aaaaaaah!

Christmas is fast approaching, and we are going to share it with Darrens' mom and dad. It will be wonderful for us all, especially Beverley. We can have a Christmas tree, which she can decorate with her nan, as we did in France. Except , that then, we would walk into our own forest and choose a tree. This year I think it will be artificial! You can't have everything… Remembering --- …. In fact last Christmas our tree was artificial too. It stood about eight inches high, with a set of tiny lights, run by an AA battery, it fitted into the Landy a treat!

Back up to Perth to await nan and grandads flight, so wonderful to see them come through the doors. I am trying to hold back the tears, wishing I wasn't quite so emotional.

Everybody settles in and it's so good to be together. The heat is a bit much so we buy an air conditioner, to stop them melting into the settee. We visit friends and all the local places that we had showed to David..

Christmas couldn't be better. We have a bbq on the beach, only marred by the thousands of flies that want to join in.

We get a phone call from Karen and Kev, whom we met in Mongolia. They are travelling around the world on their motorcycle (guzzieoverland.com). We stopped and had tea with them several times on our journey, swapped e-mails and asked them to look us up when they pass through Australia. They arrive and stop with us for a couple of days. We sat and chatted for hours, telling and listening to our stories. I love having a full house, it's so much fun, especially after being alone for so long.

Darrens' mom and dad leave us for a few weeks while they go travelling in a hired camper van. They go east to Melbourne, Sidney over to Brisbane. The weather is really bad for them, raining all the time. On their return to us they tell us that the camper van leaked on the beds, and was not up to standard at all. They travel all this way to be cheated by the hire company, but they didn't let it spoil the journey. After a couple of weeks they leave to go home, holding back the tears again, but I'm sure they'll be back.

We are still visiting Bridgetown at the week-ends, and have met so many people. It is beautifully green here, there are rolling hills and forests all around.

Darren has found work on a mine. This is thanks to Roger who gave Darren a contact phone number. He will be doing a fly in and fly out shift, two weeks away and one at home. So we have made the momentous decision to move away from Bunbury and the sea, hope it's not permanent, but it's what Darren wants. By doing this we will be close to our new freinds (but not the sea),

On a Monday morning in February we move into our friends rental house. A very pretty house with a Lemon tree in the front garden, surrounded by a white picket fence, overlooking the town. One large bedroom for us, the second bedroom leads into the third, this has been taken over by Beverley. The open plan living area includes the kitchen and dining area, with opening, floor to ceiling windows at both ends.

The whole area has been fitted with wooden walls and ceiling, very nice. Back to renting is not the independent life I crave, but maybe he's right?

Tomorrow Darren is to fly out from Perth for his first shift. It's a good feeling to know that me and Beverley are not alone, we have friends and people to call on. The first thing that happens is Beverley joins the youth theatre. This is thanks to Lucie who signs her up immediately. After spending so long without young people around her, this is quite a mammoth day for Beverley. She copes extremely well and after a few weeks she has a boyfriend, it's wonderful to see her so happy. He goes to the local school, most days she walks up to meet him, they seem to get on so well, and want to spend all their time together.

Darren has been away just a couple of days and our first crisis happens. The main water pipe has burst, water is pouring out into the front garden. I need to turn the mains off, but where is it? Where are our tools, they must be at Lucie and Andres', this is not good, I hear Mark next door, working in his garden, so I ask for help. He actually has a pair of pliers in his hands and straight away he turns off the mains, stopping the water and the meter which is spinning out of control. Next he digs out the broken pipe, sees what parts he needs, jumps in his car to fetch them, returns and fixes it. What can you say!

Now it's my turn, I have also joined the local theatre and I'm making friends and having a ball. I'm asked to be the assistant production manager on the next performance which is a winter celebration involving sketches and a pantomime with the children. Now I can meet lots of the local children, wonderful. Beverley has a part too, of course, so we can be together, whilst both doing our own thing.

July 2012. It's a cold winter this year and we find ourselves lighting the fire. Seems even more like France. I thought I would never have to split wood again, shows how naïve I can be. Bridgetown is affectionately known as Fridgetown and now I know why, although it is nothing like the cold winter of France or England. By the afternoon the temperatures are very pleasant. Looking out my front window I can see the lemon tree weighted down with fruit and the peach tree covered in blossom. In the back garden there is an olive tree, and I've managed to find a handful of delicious black olives. Next to this is a small, young mandarin tree giving miniature fruit.

If you ever find yourself in Bridgetown, ask around for us, there's a pot of tea on the stove for you!!

Nice thought, but I have to retract that offer, as me and Beverley have moved on, but that's another story!!!!!!!!!!

Printed in Great Britain
by Amazon